Born to be Free

The Freedom You Look For
Is Where You Look From

Jac O' Keeffe

Strategic Book Publishing
New York, New York

Strategic Book Publishing
An imprint of AEG Publishing Group
845 Third Avenue, 6th Floor—6016
New York, NY 10022
http://www.strategicbookpublishing.com

ISBN: 978-1-60693-397-8, 1-60693-397-3

Printed in the United States of America

Dedicated to the memory of Catherine Kelly

CONTENTS

PREFACE

Born to be Free was not written with the intention of being a literary achievement. You may dislike the tone, the language, and expressions that are used, but do not discard this book or give up on its message on these accounts. Remain with it and expect your mind to present every reason for you to reject this material. Delivery is only important to your intellect. Let the truth of what is indicated resonate with you, and your own inner knowing can then be the judge of what is written.

Resistance to knowing who you are, beyond your ideas and beliefs, will present and re-present during your reading of this book.

Take it chapter by chapter and be open to a re-read as you go, especially if you do not grasp the content at the outset. Do not expect to read this book over a weekend. If you do, what it offers will be lost to you.

INTRODUCTION

This book shines a bright light on a most direct path to unlimited and permanent happiness. It offers the reader an opportunity to understand the truth of what it is to be human, and the simplicity of what it means to live life in freedom and joy. Right here, right now, you can settle into your most natural state—that which enjoys uninterrupted peace of mind and liberation in your heart. The undisputable truth underpinning all that is can be recognised by you in one moment. This little book contains the biggest message that can exist: it directs your attention to the essence of who and what you are.

The ability to intellectually understand truth is the privilege of all comprehending adults. However, the embodiment and inner realisation that leads to an undisputable recognition of truth cannot be delivered by any book, seminar or teacher. To this end, this publication is not different in that regard, but what is here available in your hands is a clear, step by step explanation of all that is—and your part in that play of things. How you embrace this material is your choice. Should you have an eagerness to know the ultimate truth, then simply follow the signposts herein. Take every practical step that is indicated and all suffering will cease. Joy, peace, and happiness will arise from within you. If you have the courage to fully engage with what is presented you will discover yourself as you really are. In this discovery, nothing can inhibit your recognition of your true nature and you shall return to your harmonious, natural state of being.

Chapter 1
HAPPINESS

What does it take for you to be happy? Do you touch into happiness for brief moments or do you have periods of sustained happiness? Is happiness a feeling out there in your future that you believe you will eventually attain? Do you have a formula in your mind that is the recipe for your happiness? When you fulfil that formula will you really be happy and, most importantly, will it last?

Is this happiness a consequence of finding the right partner, lover, house or job? If you believe that happiness is awaiting you in your future, then rest assured it will never come. Be prepared for a long wait, for that is simply an idea in your mind that keeps happiness at arm's length. Happiness is a direct experience arising from your innate nature. The origin of happiness rests completely outside the perimeters of your mind.

Your mind has no capacity to embrace, engage, or interpret real and permanent happiness. A feel-good experience or temporary pleasure is not happiness. The happiness that every person can enjoy is of a permanent, unchanging and undisturbable nature.

If you can say that you have never been happy in your life, then you must know what happiness is in order to recognise that you do not feel it. Unlike other methods and techniques, a simple path towards understanding what happiness is, is offered here to you. The keys to living in the freedom of absolute happiness are in your physical hands right now.

Does your mind hold the opinion that you are not entitled to feel happy? Some people deny themselves happiness because there is too much suffering in the world. Others believe there is value in punishing themselves for acts in their past. Perhaps you believe that happiness is something that other people enjoy but somehow it does not happen for you. All of these reasonings are constructs of the human mind, serving only to keep happiness at bay.

Achieving personal and professional goals brings a relative satisfaction. Some people appear to have it all—a wonderful partner, attractive lifestyle, material wealth and so on. But, as things in life become more familiar, they generally become less entertaining. Every new addition to one's life offers a distraction for a while, but the novelty phase associated with each personal or professional achievement comes to an end sooner or later. At the point of noticing this pattern, one recognises that to set up another goal would simply lead to the same place—that place of inner dissatisfaction and emptiness. The search for happiness continues.

There is no readily accessible model in our modern world that tells us about real and permanent happiness. In this commercially driven, economically progressive era, the innate human thirst for happiness is cleverly exploited by commerce for its own ends. The sophisticated modern mind has created a concept of happiness, as if it is something each of us should apply effort to attain. Many believe that stepping out of their social status momentum would mean they would lose their chance for happiness. What would become of those who believe that to drop out means you cannot keep up with the pace and so you must be a loser? That defines one game of life, if you choose to play it in that way. There are many ways to play out your life. Take a moment to see if you want to write your script yourself or do you want society or another external influence to write it for you? This is your choice. Whether you exercise it or not, recognise at this point that the choice is yours to make.

So what is happiness for you? Is happiness what you feel when you are going on a holiday, playing with your children, gardening, out on the golf course or having a drink on a Friday evening? If happiness depends on an external influence for you to experience it, then you are not feeling happiness. External circumstances that allow you to enjoy a good feeling when relieved from pressures of work, when you step out of your mind and relax with alcohol, are in nature, or playing with children cannot induce true happiness. These escapes from your normal day-to-day experience present valuable distractions and are a source of pleasure and relaxation but happiness is a different thing.

For example, you may believe that you would be happy if you had a house beside the sea. This belief can develop into a desire and you can focus on achieving it. When you realise that goal and get your house beside the sea, this desire naturally subsides and allows a natural stillness to arise in your mind. You may even think you are happy now that this desire is fulfilled. However, this happiness is short lived. Why? It is not in the nature, characteristics or the properties of a house beside the sea to afford happiness to its dwellers. A house, no matter where it's located, does not have the capacity to give happiness. If it did, then it would follow that all people would find the same level of happiness in having that object. In contrast, some will find the same property conjures feelings of loneliness and isolation. The quality of happiness is not in the nature of any object. So if a house beside the sea is not responsible for making you happy, where does this feeling of happiness come from when you initially acquire that desired object?

Happiness arises from within. It is a quality of your innate nature. Thoughts distract you from consciously abiding in and enjoying your innate nature. Thoughts create all desires and desires can be all-consuming. Your mind can convince you that attaining a particular object of desire will make you happy. The truth is that when your mind is still, a natural feeling of happiness arises within you. Your true nature is causeless and living causeless happiness is your natural state of being. When a desire is satisfied, the desire subsides and mind rests for a period. The absence of desire, the absence of thought, allows what is within to be experienced.

An unmanaged mind presents another desire soon. This in turn convinces you that you can revive your subsiding state of happiness by attaining another detail that will make it all perfect again! This state of temporary happiness can be enjoyed with the subsidence of desires. Yet, within the state of happiness, there is a moment of causeless happiness. But the mind very quickly takes over and offers an objective cause and the cycle of anticipating a repetition of the state of happiness begins again. Managing desire and your mind, which is the source of desire, yields an opportunity to rest in and enjoy the innate happiness abiding always. Happiness is natural and does not require support of desires, thoughts, emotions, effort, goals, or finances!

The feeling experience of happiness does not change according to external circumstances; it is not contingent on extraneous human living. It is within us all, dormant perhaps, but innate to human life force. Happiness exists independently of external circumstances. To say that you were happy until your husband died is not understanding happiness. That is not happiness because happiness cannot be given or taken away by anything that life throws at you. It is internal, unchanging, and constant. It is still, it is calm, and it is complete. It searches for nothing, it does not seek anything, it is absolute, and it is. Your access to it is in your capacity to be still, to relax, and to stop engaging with your thinking. Thus the only thing that can stop you from feeling happiness is you.

To continue to look outside for something that is already inside only serves to distract you from looking within. There is a fundamental flaw in the pursuit of happiness. It can never be attained from without and so to pursue it in any way is futile. The very idea of a quest for happiness is a misnomer. Happiness is a natural rhythm within you and, as long as you trawl the mind and desires in search of it, you will not find it. All external circumstances, activities, possessions and events are designed to keep the mind entertained. But happiness is outside the realm of the mind; it is outside the functionings and capacity of the mind. It is in the realm of placing your attention on your innate nature. To feel and experience real happiness, causeless happiness, requires a conscious or unconscious surrendering of your interest in your thoughts.

On arriving at that point of knowing that physical things or people or situations cannot make you happy there are possibilities for where to step forward. Many increase pressure on their relationships, expecting more than the relationship is designed to yield. Some look for an other that may offer a more exciting sexual distraction. These options present their own consequences. Others arrive at a place labelled depression, presented as disillusionment with life. The meaningless of everything has become evident. When nothing satisfies, general motivation to live lessens. In truth, this is a moment to be celebrated. The search for purpose and meaning is now ripe to begin.

A choice is presented. You can take a good and honest look at life and face the hard questions about the purpose and meaning of your life. You can go further and ask what and who you are. Thus, you may begin to feel and address a yearning to know the truth. This involves taking a risk and entering unknown territory that will bring change. The only other option is to continue as before, accepting that the world does not satisfy and, when emotional pain gets too much to bear, alcohol and/or drugs, recreational or pharmaceutical, are society's answers to this naturally occurring yearning for understanding, spiritual knowledge and happiness.

Arriving at the place where you know that there must be more to life and to you is an opening, not a dead end. Your choice to walk through this opening must be made in total awareness; this is not a rabbit hole that you can peep into before deciding if you will enter. The choice is simple; take a risk or continue as is and play it safe.

This book is filled with signposts to assist you in sourcing and resting within that deepest part of who you are. If you choose you can work this material and make real change happen within you. This will result in your life changing externally to some extent and internally to a greater extent. Be prepared to let the consequences take care of themselves. Everything will work out for the good of all when you walk the path towards understanding truth. It always does.

If you are simply curious, your mind will remain in charge and it will judge this material as an intellectual or academic exercise and lose its potential for you. Are you someone who likes to process and analyse information as soon as it comes to your attention? Does this method generally lead you to understanding? In and of itself, that can be a very effective system. Many who take in new ideas in this way process information only and never take that step towards practising the material. The mind likes the feeling of understanding ideas— rejecting or accepting them as it sees fit—and it is momentarily satisfied. It is the nature of the intellect to doubt, so doubts regarding this material will arise and the cycle begins again as the intellect looks for another stimulus to give another temporary hit. All through this process, the mind is in charge. In the natural cerebral pause, before the onset of doubt, most do not take the next step to set the mind aside and actually try out the suggested signposts. Spiritual practise involves actively ignoring the mind. It initially involves a doing, an action, a practise outside of the normal realm of mind. Expect your mind to be filled with resistance. To practise this material means to relax and surrender the mind with all of its skills and concepts. They are of little use within the spiritual domain.

As one starting point, have you considered that some place within you recognises happiness? If you know what happiness is not, then maybe you might know what it is. All people have a sense that the capacity to feel happiness is within them, and some have experienced it. This path towards truth leads to happiness and more. There is much that lies beyond your mind, so do not limit yourself to the desire for feeling happy, but see where this road can lead.

At the core, this book invites you to explore who you are beyond your mind, beyond the identity that your family and society has placed on you and that you have placed on yourself. Who are you when you expose the deeper and secret parts of yourself to yourself? Who are you when you go beyond the murky unsavouries? Be totally honest with yourself. Maybe there is kindness and a calm and peaceful nature under the recesses of all else within you. Let us see what you find. All of this leads to a place beyond your mind, so be prepared to know that you are not your thoughts. You have thoughts. The number is estimated to be in the region of 90,000 daily. But they are not you and do not define you. Let us see what there really is to you when you peel back all of your experiences and suffering, and all the memories that may be over-active when they better belong at rest and ignored with the distant past. Experiences are very valid at the time when they occur; they brought us to this point. But let that be their total value. Don't drag them around like a comfort blanket, but glean their best use and be present to who you are in this moment. Your mind will use any material from your life to draw your attention from the present moment. Mind does not exercise quality control; it will throw up stories and feelings from your past or imagined future to prevent you from directing your attention elsewhere. Mind constantly presents the past or future as present. As you walk this road within, exploring the questions of who you are and what are you doing on this planet, your mind is quickly out of its depth. It will make every effort to distract you and pull you back to what it calls "real life." I put it to you that your mind has no sense of what ultimate reality is, your mind is a tool to help you function effectively in this world and it is limited to that function. The questions that you may have, that lie beyond day-to-day living, science and philosophy, can all be answered from within you. Yes, all of them, but it requires throwing out thoughts and concepts that you may hold dear. If you are willing then, let's go!

Chapter 2
EXPERIENCE

In asking yourself who you are, it is natural that your mind presents a complete personal and social profile. It may offer an identity that has a valuable currency within the external reality of society. To this end, it may present your name, age, sex, education and training, occupation, marital status, personality traits, nationality, religious beliefs etc. Is this who you are? Or is this the persona that you consent to represent you, consciously and unconsciously, to give you a way to meet family, society and your community? Of course, this has value and probably has taken quite an investment to create. However, if you are asking questions about purpose and meaning, this definition does not suffice. Then, is there an external you and an internal you? A private and a public person? I put it to you that both are creations of your mind. Both are established from the same database as every other thinking person on the planet and are according to what you deem as safe. There is a line as to what can or cannot be exposed.

The private and personal identity of each person relies on memory. This is where we store emotional thoughts, desires, old wounds and grudges, listings of those who have hurt us, pains we have caused, fears and more. We hold onto memories of love lost. We retain memories and stories of opportunities that we missed by a hairline—had circumstances been different, they could have changed everything. Such thoughts from the past pose as current experience and influence our perception of the future. Fears about financial security, fear for ourselves, our safety, the planet, the afterlife, the listings are endless and your mixed bag may not be that different than mine. Whatever your mind chews on in the dark of a sleepless night is most likely the imprint of subject matter that was laid during your childhood.

Many life experiences that happened to us as children gave rise to damaged and low self-esteem levels. Such experiences include being forced to participate in events that you knew you were not good at and then put down for performing badly, being made to feel that your opinion was worthless and/or stupid, repeatedly not being listened to, feeling unsafe in the company of an adult who was responsible for you, being the recipient of sexual abuse, physical abuse etc. Such experiences are part of life for many. However, if you feel an emotional response when you think of these or any unsavoury event in your past, it is a clear indicator that letting go still needs to take place. Expending emotional energy into a memory or a fear about your future depletes your health and crushes self-confidence. Abusive childhood experiences can damage and destroy self-esteem. However, every wound, every emotion, linked to experiences in the past can be released when you are ready to do so.

People react in different ways. It is not so much the experiences we have had in early life that is important, but how we respond to them and how we integrate these experiences into our life. Those who come through relatively unscathed have a solid sense of who they are. They understand and accept that experiences happen as part of life and are generally not taken personally.

For others who grapple to find some solid footing as a coping mechanism, experiences are internalised and used to inform themselves of who they are. For example, a child may deduce that if I am beaten, this must mean that I am bad. Thus the pattern of identifying with an experience takes place and causes a person to be emotionally sensitive in adult life. As a consequence, everything that happens is about me, telling me if I am good or bad, right or wrong, okay or not okay. Many have a heightened sensitivity to the responses of others and believe that all interactions in daily life tell them something about themselves. For example, if someone walks past Terry on the street and seems to ignore him, he instantly believes that he must have upset them in some way. Terry does not consider options that may have caused the person to ignore Terry. He never considers that the person was preoccupied, distracted, having a bad day or just did not want to communicate. Because of the way Terry's mind works, all Terry's experiences inform him of who he is, how he is and if he is going to be accepted or not. Each situation bares its own threat and promise. With this way of thinking, it is not possible to allow for another person to have their life continue independently to his. Everything is about Terry. So everything has the potential to cause emotional hurt. The mind without editing draws its own conclusion about every experience. This way of processing happenings in daily life leads to pain and suffering. Mind operating in this way is a symptom of poor self-esteem. The mind can be retrained to stop using external circumstances and experiences to tell a person, in this case Terry, who he is. We want the world to be all about us when we have not consciously realised the truth of who we are. We seek external guidelines to compensate when we fail to make that internal connection. This mental pattern never finds its conclusion. It knows no rest and will never bring redemption. It only leads to pain and suffering. It is a pattern that must be seen for what it is and in the seeing it will drop automatically. Thus it can be transcended, not resolved. This pattern of behaviour arises when the mind draws on experiences from the past to offer an unneeded reference point in order to interpret events in the present.

It is the nature of your mind to present you with thoughts and to seek experiences. The purpose of experience is to offer you the opportunity to engage with life. They are simply experiences. They are not loaded with meanings and indications of who you are and how the world works. Misinterpretation is made subjectively by you, the thinker, and can mislead. It always leads to temporary pleasure and seemingly unending cycles of pain and suffering. Experiences cannot change anything: they only have the power to do so if you give it. Experiences come and go, but their impact on you is determined solely by your level of identification with them. For example, if you deduce that something happened to you because you were a bad person, that is your mind identifying with events and seeking to find out more about you from your experiences. In this case, your mind held a belief that you were bad and you used this belief to interpret an otherwise benign experience to reaffirm a subjective belief. But your experiences cannot tell you who you are; they do not define you in any way. If you think they do, you have confused your identity with your ability to experience. Every experience is there for your participation. We generally learn as we go. But, believing that an experience can impact on who you are is simply not true. Experiences can damage your body or reduce your confidence, but the facility to experience enables you to enjoy and participate in being human. You are not that which you experience. Only the concepts that you hold about yourself to be true can be influenced by your experiences. There is an essential essence, a core within you that is not touchable by any experience. This core essence does not identify with any event, person or place in your life. This is why you cannot be damaged beyond repair by any event that has ever happened to you. This is why happiness cannot be affected by exterior circumstances; happiness is a fragrance rising from this core essence. This is who you really are.

If you have been holding onto emotional trauma, no matter how horrific, and even if you have been told by a therapist that you may never get over such trauma, know that this is totally false. Experiences do not change anything that is real or permanent; your essence cannot be affected. Your mind may believe you are tainted to the core, but this is not possible. You are not a victim of your experiences. You lived through experiences and you can live with their memory. Know that the experience is not who you are and flow with the idea that the emotional pain attached to a memory can begin to release. You will find that you do not need emotions attached to memories if you know that you cannot glean your identity from your experiences. Let feelings from a memory surface, then let them go without resistance. Your memory records stories in a benign manner. All experiences are limited, all memories are limited. Emotions are limited, finite expressions. They are not to be feared but allowed as part of the diversity of what life can offer to us feeling beings. There is no painful emotion that arises without your mind first having a thought. Through electrical impulse, thought stimulates your body to produce chemicals that give rise to emotion. Thus human emotions are a by-product of your thinking. If assistance is needed there are effective techniques available that help release painful or paralysing emotions.

Examine yourself to determine to what extent you draw on your experiences, memories, and beliefs as reference points for your current behaviour. If you bring your past into the present, it distorts your experience of each new day. Try to bring objectivity, a freshness to your perspective—this is what is meant by being fully present or being in the moment. This may appear simplistic, but the truth is that if you pay no attention to your memories they cannot touch you because without thought, they cease to be alive for you. There is nothing to be gained from holding onto pain except more pain.

An experience is a happening coupled with a reaction that received your attention to find expression. There is nothing more to an experience. Do not fall into the trap of giving it more importance. Let the past rest in the past. Memories are like a drug. They alter your awareness of the present by bringing your attention to a series of self-created personal recordings from the past. A past that is located where? Does the past even exist? The past does not exist: neither does the future exist.

These are only concepts. If these concepts hold your attention through stories, you will suffer.

Believing that you can select nice memories and discard those that bring discomfort is a trick of the mind. If you focus on memory, consciously or unconsciously, the good memories will come with the bad. This is because when mind is in the habit of gleaning personal identity from experiences, it does so without discrimination.

Experiences are something that you had. They are not what or who you are. You will only create suffering opportunities for yourself if you use them to make you feel special or different. Again, this is seeking of identity through experiences, an interpretation of mind that leads to continued suffering. Your true identity lies much deeper than any experience that life has presented you. If you have survived the most horrendous ordeal, this does not make you special. It has nothing to do with who you are: it simply means that you survived something out of the ordinary, nothing more. The experience is over, allow life to go on. Life continues anyway, whether or not you are attentively present in it as it unfolds.

If you have been using experiences to determine how you feel about yourself, to gauge how you are doing, and if you are ready to stop this misleading pattern, then you will need to affirm your sense of self and self-worth. Now, experiences can be just experiences, and who you are stands alone independently of the happenings of each day. There is an immense liberation in this internal shift. Your natural state is one of calm, peace, joy, relaxed ease and happiness. You can and will discover this for yourself. All is within you. An outward-looking mind cannot engage in such an inner enquiry. In order to find out who you are and to live from your natural state, your mind must be guided in an about turn.

Let us take a look at self-esteem in order to give a perspective on shifting a belief system you may have adopted regarding who or what you are. If your private mental chatter is generally turbulent and disturbing, this indicates emotional insecurity and low self-esteem. While intact self-esteem is not actually necessary for self-enquiry, it certainly helps. It closes the door on many distractions that impede living consciously from your natural state of calm and ease. A good starting point is checking in to see how your relationship is with yourself. If you choose to stop looking to others to find out about you, self-acceptance arises. Now an external gauge is not needed. Essentially, if your self-esteem is intact, you have no reason to turn yourself inside out for self-confirmation and approval. You can decide to leave this package of exhausting work to the side if you now realise that it is a redundant activity.

Your level of self-esteem rests on two corner-stones; knowing that you are lovable and knowing that you are capable. If you do not believe that you are lovable, you have choice. You can hold onto a wound caged within a memory that may have taught you that you were not lovable. Or you can see that those who influenced your belief that you were not lovable were acting out of their own pain. Perhaps in this situation, what others did or said was about them and not about you. If you have an objective perspective on your memories, you will see that this is generally the case. Do you want to continue to believe someone else's opinion or do you want to really see if you are lovable? Even if you never felt loved, this has nothing to do with being lovable. This is a condition that exists outside of having someone to love you. You can live alone on a deserted island and be lovable. If you are isolated in your life right now, can you still see the truth? Can you understand that you are lovable? It is a condition natural to being human. Can you allow yourself to feel it? The choice is yours. You might continue to berate yourself to prolong suffering and enjoy the wallowing that self-pity allows, continuing with the old identity. Or are you able to accept that you are lovable?

The second pillar to self-esteem asks if you know that are you capable. This does not question whether the world thinks you are capable. I am not asking you for evidence that you are a capable employer, worker, parent, friend, lover etc. This question is not answered by looking at the world or to any external experience for verification. In this instance being capable does not refer to a skills base. It rests on the belief that you have the capacity and the ability to take action when required. Being capable means knowing that you are not helpless and that you have the ability to respond to what life presents on a daily basis. This is what makes us capable. This is nothing to do with whether you decide to exercise your capabilities or not. Deep within you, without searching for evidence, do you believe, do you know that you are a capable person? Do you have that self-worth? Are you capable of a deeper inner enquiry than what you have made to date? Can you accept the possibility that right now you are able to look deeper within? Know that this ability has underpinned your reading of this book.

If you know you are capable, it means you have a sense of self-worth. It means that within you there is a value that you have and that you are capable. It is likely that your mind will resist this. Because to connect with your essence, which is by its very nature love and ability, you will no longer use your mind to filter experiences to tell you if you are lovable and capable. So your mind will fight for its very existence here. Your mind likes to keep busy and to be the king, governing your every aspect in a kingdom where it has no place.

Every person is lovable and capable, as these qualities are not necessarily earned or accumulated. This is because being lovable and capable are human expressions of your essential nature. You can operate from that deeper part of you—knowing and accepting your human nature. Or you can view the world from the old paradigm that is the subjective position of your mind. If you hold fast to your old beliefs, you will continue to be emotionally-sensitive to some degree and draw conclusions from every experience. Thus you will invariably create invalid thoughts and ideas about people and situations in order to make yourself feel okay and that you got it right. Why do we do this to ourselves? Because many find their place in the world from a mixed bag of memories they drag around and lean on for identity and reference. Remember that your experiences brought you here; that was their purpose. You can revisit them in turbulent moments in your mind or with professional help, but at the end of the day you are still faced with the same choice; drag them with you or arrive at a point of knowing that you have had enough and begin to let them go. Memories arise and fall. When your attention is not involved in the stories they present, they naturally subside into the past. Let them remain there. The choice is yours to make. Right now is a good time to choose. Who you are in this very moment is who you are, and there is no point in fooling yourself into thinking otherwise. Can you afford to stop berating yourself and feel that, deep within, you are lovable and capable? With no evidence to support this, can you feel that these qualities arise from your core? If a leap of faith is required here, then take it.

If you choose to stay with the old paradigm and want to believe that you are not lovable or capable, then you will remain with that understanding of yourself. Consider exploring the possibility of actually finding out if what you believe about yourself is the truth. Put your beliefs to the test and examine the supporting evidence honestly to uncover the truth. If you decide to keep your investment in the past, nothing will change. The rest of this book will only present theory. Doing whatever you need to do to get a sense of truth will open an internal door for you: a door into that real nature which is beyond your mind, a door towards discovering who or what you really are. Avoid comparing levels of lovability and capability to that of others; mind projects outward out of habit and comparisons can negate your self-worth. You are not being asked to change your situation or any aspect of your life. You are asked to change your mind about the impact that your past experiences now have on you, that is all. The advantage to this step is that it allows you to unplug from your mind, in self-acceptance, so you can focus attention on the tricks of your mind and see what lies beyond it, instead of being victim to the concepts it presents.

People with high self-esteem generally move forward and accept these ideas quickly. Persons with low self-esteem have less of a belief that they can change. The investment in their past is greater and so their resistance is stronger. If you are looking for the truth about yourself, about life and its meaning, then have no fear: this path is light and full of freedom. But it does require you to take risks. So let's look at fear, as fear may now raise its head and present you with convincing resistance.

We learned about fear as children. Many of us learned that the world is an unsafe place. We may have learned that we are not protected, listened to, understood, or respected. What you learned is stored as information in your mind. You can choose to believe it or not. Because it was hard earned is no reason to keep it alive. Liberation rests in letting it go. No matter how much every lesson was repeated, if it taught you to fear, it is now useless.

There is nothing to fear, ever. If you continue to place attention on fear-creating ideas, knowing that your thoughts create emotions, you will feel fear. In a moment, you can decide that enough is enough and end your pattern of feeling fear.

What is required of you to live without fear? Trust. Nothing more than trust. If you think you don't know how to trust, remind yourself what it feels like to trust things that you do trust. For example, you trust that the sun will rise tomorrow, you trust that when you answer the phone you will remember how to speak, you trust that you will remember to put your clothes on before you leave your home in the morning. You trust all of the time. Those places where you have applied this trust flow smoothly and happen without you doing anything. The sun rises, you are able to communicate, you get prepared for the day, trust brings a flow. There is nothing to fear when you trust the unfolding of life. Whatever is presented, no matter the scale, you will respond then, as it happens.

Chapter 3
OBSERVE

Shining a light on patterns of thinking and conditioned beliefs held in the human mind is necessary in order to start the adventure of finding out who you are. The easiest, obvious, and yet most potent place to begin is through understanding the subtleties of your mind. If you do not know yourself in this way and cannot see the creations of your own mind, then how can you change? How can anything change? Without this self-knowledge you are a prisoner of your restrictive thoughts, beliefs and values. In any moment, if you are not content and at peace with total certainty, you can know that your mind has created this situation. Nothing outside of you has the power to impact on you in any way. It is your thoughts and ideas about the external world and your reactions to it that create the undesired effect.

As your understanding of your own mind increases, you will recognise its tricks, its convincing arguments, and its ideas of how the world should be. Your mind believes that if things went according to what you believe to be the right way then everything would be fine. This is not the truth. This is a game your mind uses to keep you resisting what is. Essentially, it is a construct created to give you that good feeling that you are right and that you know what is best. Your mind loves to be right. It gains satisfaction from its superiority complex, and every adult human mind has a superiority complex that will take your attention to dissolve. This, like other constructs in your thinking that you may have noticed, is a futile attempt to make you feel whole. The mind was never designed to fulfil that objective, because the desire to feel whole is the call from your deeper self to look within.

Without seeing your mind at play and looking at what is happening, there is no chance of attaining self-knowledge. You will continue to be a prisoner of your thoughts and a slave of your mind. Either you are in charge or your conditioned thinking is in charge. At any given moment, you have the option to connect with your subjective beliefs and personal thoughts, with the world and all its events; or to freely flow with what is presented. There is no halfway house, no interim perspective: every moment presents to you a fresh opportunity.

Perhaps you have observed your mind for some time, or you may be beginning to do so now. Observing in this way is to develop an awareness in that you can see your thoughts arise and fall without identifying with them and buying the story they present, as if it were the undisputed truth of how things are. It allows you to live from the viewpoint where you see your mind impartially and do not defend it. Rather, you can see humour in how crazy your thinking can be: this is when the wake-up call has begun. The awakening from this dream state of believing your thoughts has had its initial stirrings and another level of consciousness is accessible to you now.

If you can recognise that you are thinking, and observe that you are having a thought, then who is it that is observing? Who is observing your mind? Most of the time, if you are honest with yourself, you may be totally engrossed in what you see taking place in the world, at work, at home. You are in the world of your mind, seeing and reacting as one with your mind, as if you are your mind. Usually, there is no objectivity. While it may seem that life is all-engrossing, the fact is that your mind has you engrossed. Life is busy at times, calm at times, stressful much of the time, and all these ideas about life are created through the mind. Life is none of these things. However, your mind interprets and judges life as such, so that it has a larger volume of beliefs, ideas and material to like and dislike. The mind judges and reacts emotionally. It decides there is too much pressure and creates stress, thinking this can enable you to move faster and respond quicker. However, the optimum way to manage daily events in life is to self-manage. Step back from your mind's interpretation of all that is taking place in front of you. See it from an objective perspective without engaging your mind. You will not interpret events on a personal level and will therefore be more present and clearly available to what is actually taking place. The shift is from personal to impersonal. Instead of events happening to you and taking everything personally, they simply happen. All takes place around you. Your connection with events can be impersonal and nothing happens to you. You will soon begin to notice order and a natural flow to all things. You will find this to be true even if what is happening is stressful.

No situations can happen in life in which you need your identifying mind to respond. Every situation has a flow and a sequence. Awareness sees this, but the thinking mind generally cannot. It does not have that skill. Decision-making takes place without the thinking mind. Sitting quietly yields answers in its own time. With patience and calmness, direction will come from within. Your mind uses many hooks to keep itself in charge of your day; it will not surrender easily. This is why the practice of viewing the world through the eyes of your observing self is necessary. It is also why it requires conscious application in the beginning.

Not using your mind for personal identification with the thoughts it presents brings an end to suffering and allows a great unburdening to take place. It does not mean that you will become stupid or disconnected from daily events. Quite the opposite experience unfolds in that a clear objectivity in every moment is accessible to you. The flow of what is, is not disturbed by the personal idea that things should be another way. Freedom from this thought alone yields immunity from attitudinal inflexibility, stubbornness, and self-righteousness. All that is required is a shift in perspective through removing a personal agenda. Do not buy the idea that events are all about you. Drop the mental connection between who, how, what you are and daily life. Let your attention be on what is taking place, not on how you fear it may impact on you. Such a perspective is the functioning capacity of the observer of your personal mind.

The observer is impartial and honest. If you think you have not experienced your observer, can you imagine that you are standing in front of you, looking at you reading this book? Go on: in your mind, stand out there and look and notice this person who is actually the physical you—reading. Get a feel of the observer part of you looking on. As you stand looking, observe with no feeling, no emotions, just look and be still. If you can do that, it is a sample of how the observer functions—without reaction. If you could do that, did you notice that there were no thoughts while you observed? The observer does not think, it does not need to. The observer knows, without knowing that it knows. It knows how to manage a crisis, it knows and sees the optimum outcome impartially: it has wisdom beyond the imaginings of the doubting mind. In this example your observer notices what is and no more. However, we are not compartmentalised in this way and the observer must function within you and look at life through your eyes. The observer does not have the store of conditioned thoughts the mind has and it has access to much more. It has intuition and wisdom, it is relaxed and flows with what is. It knows that nothing in life can throw you, it knows no fear. In contrast, the identifying mind thinks that many things in life can and perhaps will throw you and it fears. The observer is a doorway to a much, much deeper part of you. It is the access point to the infinite within you and to the beyond infinite you.

Of course the observer is mind also, but it does not identify with things, people, events and stories. It is said that the observer is "I AM" which offers a clear understanding in that the observer exists but it does not identify with form or state. The observer, the I AM, is the formless. It is infinite and in many ways in polarity to the thinking mind. It presents a balance so that we can see one and the other state and enjoy both as they

35

facilitate experience through contrast. The I AM is emptiness, space, and from space arises form and things. In other words, the observer, the I AM, is creator of all that can be created. However, the I AM state is not the ultimate, but it is a place of rest, of being, of no mind and of no time. The nature of the I AM is holiness. It contains no thing and cannot be spoiled. I AM has no sense of separation. Holy unity with all; a oneness can be experienced in this level of consciousness. Many reach this state in meditation as its access requires the dropping of interest in thoughts and a stilling of the mind. One can be in that state of awareness at will with practise. However, any level of awareness that you can go to with your mind, even if it is to a state of no mind, you must and will leave it again as the pull of identification with mind and body will demand further attention.

Resting in the I AM is often referred to as a spiritual experience. Many people come out of these experiences motivated by an eagerness to tell the story of what they experienced. Then identification takes over and what happened to "me" becomes more important than resting in that state of being, of no mind. It is not that one state of awareness is intrinsically better than another. They are different and together offer opportunities to experience. When you look at the world through the identifying mind, everything changes all of the time. Contrast is clearly defined through pleasure and pain. Looking from the I AM, all is objectively perceived from a relaxed stillness. This is why I AM is sometimes called universal energy or first principle.

This leads to the inevitable fact that the role of the mind must be reassessed, and you can only do this for you as your thinking mind is a subjective thing and the thoughts it entertains are your responsibility. You alone have access to the workings of your mind. What is in evidence on the broader scale is that the beautiful and exquisite human mind is an invaluable resource to every human being. It is a key instrument facilitating us to live a human life. The human mind seeks many things, including purpose, meaning, information and affirmation. In many, it desires activity, distraction and stimulation continually. Should it be untamed and misunderstood in its functions and limitations, it will exercise its capacity to control many aspects of your life. It has tremendous use, but it is limited because its nature and function are finite. In the main, it accumulates knowledge and information only from other minds. Its nature is to doubt and so it constantly seeks information, dissects, analyses and, before long, seeks new information. It constantly recycles concepts on a competitive circuit of limitation. This begins to change when one shifts an outward looking mind to having an inward focus. Being less interested in what the world of form offers and seeking to find some satisfying answers creates this turn around.

Underpinning all functions of the mind is its perception and acceptance of the concept of separation. When it identifies with one thing, it automatically rejects another, hence separation. The human mind sees the world in a separate and dualistic way. It believes I am me and you are you, and that we are separate human beings on every level. The mind purports that some things are good and some things are bad, there is right and there is wrong, judgement prevails and where judgement takes place there is always separation as an inherent value. It views the world from a dualistic perspective. Mind is subjective and reactive. It uses experiences of life to feed you with a certain knowledge and a limited understanding that helps greatly in day-to-day living. However, if mind yields to no mind and the calm observer holds your attention, you would manage at least as well in an average day.

Your mind has a competitive nature and, because of this, it always seeks to gauge how you are doing emotionally, physically, intellectually, even spiritually by comparing you to others. It is competitive at its core and competition is only possible where unity is not perceived. Unity is a concept and is known and understood by the observer, so it is not necessary to turn your mind inside out teaching it new concepts. Better to dissolve and remove existing concepts at every opportunity. The interconnectedness of all things often does not make sense to people who do not engage their observer consciously. People have told me that they hear that "all is one" as a theory, but they do not feel how it can be so. When you practise being in the impersonal observer state of awareness, the unity of all things makes perfect sense. But the unity concept can never be fully grasped by the thinking mind, as mind bases all its beliefs on separation being reality. Once you experience and feel the formless, mind surrenders to the greater wisdom and knowing of the observer. The mind thinks and the observer knows. Therefore one key at this point is to know when to use your thinking mind and when to engage your observer self; the former is useful for planning and limited practical application. Another key is to be responsible and manage yourself to the extent of actively remembering to drop your interest in thoughts and yield your perhaps resisting mind to oneness and the divine order that is always present. Acquiring self-knowledge will give you the wisdom and skills to evolve from gross identification with mind.

If you are unconscious of the observing capacity within you, you will not see the workings of your separate mind. There are many aspects to the mind. It is logical, creative and strategic but, for evolutionary and developmental purposes, the conditioned part of your thinking is that which we are most concerned with at this point. Over-identification with mind has lead to much suffering in the world, from wars to famines. Its belief in separation denies the unity underpinning all the planet's citizens. Mind notices difference only and always seeks to acquire more. It is concerned with having and not having. If it has more, or achieves bigger goals, it believes such things will make it more powerful and ultimately happier. Through the ages, such thinking has been a significant contributing factor that results in the present day's distribution of wealth throughout the world, as the mind can understand wealth to be power.

Until the mind is understood and managed there will be wars. Until the leaders of nations learn how to operate from their observer capacity, history will repeat itself. Politics and media are closely linked. Until inner peace becomes the desired and familiar experience of the public, turbulence and troubles will be of more interest and will sell in the media and in politics before any stories of peace and continued peace.

While the importance of managing the mind is a concept as old as humanity, it is even now only seen within the realms of personal or spiritual development. We have no model as yet in education or in health to learn about when to use and how to use the thinking mind. Without proper direction, we misuse, overuse, inappropriately use and mismanage this faculty. This is the primary cause of all suffering. Because the human mind is overrated in terms of capacity and skill, and has had little if any effective impersonal management, contemporary society now highly rewards a sharp mind. Of itself this is understandable, but it seems to follow that the mind is expected to have all the answers. It cannot: it is simply a tool. The human mind is an instrument to be used when it is needed and put aside when it is not. It is a tool like any other. Like the physical body, it is a resource to be kept alert and healthy, and thus respected. In this way, the mind can be viewed as part of what we are: its limitations can be better understood and its management can earnestly begin. Your mind was created to serve you, not to be your master.

It is wise to have unlimited patience and tolerance for your mind because its functioning is beautiful. Some tend to judge their mind, the stories it churns out, the emotional responses that come so quickly and can catch you in a saga of personal drama. When you judge the mind, you are no longer observing. If you observe, there is no reaction to the high jinks of your mind. The problem is not with the mind, it is the personal identification with thoughts that creates suffering. Every human being expresses through the personal mind until it no longer serves him to do so. Judgement of the mind represents another facet of personal drama. For all experiences of humanity are stages on the evolutionary path. There is only the path and without mind we cannot experience.

In connecting with your observer, even in a brief moment of non-identification with thought, could it be possible that my observer is different from yours? Are there qualities that my observer has that are not featured in yours? If my observer met your observer, would they have something to talk about? Would they see each other as two separate existing entities in the first place? Is there a "me" and a "you" in the realm of observer? If you spent time right now in your observer and surrendered all interest in the activity of your mind, and another was meditating, right now arriving at the same state of mind in observation, then surely there is but one I AM state of consciousness that you would both be experiencing at that moment.

For many the desire to make a difference in the lives of others or the planet motivates their life. Like everything, this has its place and plays a part in the playing out of a grand design. Making a difference is a motivation from the mind. It arises when there is a belief that things are not okay and that work needs to be undertaken to make things better, to make things right. All is well. All unfolds perfectly. This is what your observer knows. The mind plays an invaluable role in motivating people to have great and effective usefulness in the world. If making a difference is how it resonates with the person doing this work, then so be it. It is important to realise that the origin of motivation, in this case, is personal gain. At other times, actions take place that are motivated by another power that does not have its place of origin in the realm of mind. These outcomes are invariably more efficient and effective in every way. These are simply different ways of operating in the world: both are effective but the former carries the limitation of a personal agenda.

The thinking mind seeks purpose, but in truth there is no purpose to any of it. There is no purpose to your life, no purpose to creation. The mind searches for purpose, seeking to find meaning. Perhaps it will find one or two purposeful ambitions during your life. However, sooner or later, these purposes will not arrive at deep meaning and a thirst will arise for a new motivation, a new purpose. The idea of purpose is your mind searching where there is no answer of that ilk. There is no answer that will lead to the why of it all. But what there is, is usefulness. Usefulness can serve as the highest purpose if your mind seeks reasons for living and taking action. To be of use to yourself, others and to the planet is the only reason, at this point. There are many ways that you can be of use. You have the freedom and privilege to choose in what way you would like and enjoy being of use. It can be fulfilling to the human experience to be of use. It is not that being of use is a good thing or a bad thing, but simply why not?

Chapter 4
SPIRITUALITY

The guiding principle that underpins a spiritual life is having a primary concern with a deeper enquiry to find the absolute truth. If you are committed to this enquiry, then know that only you can take these steps. You cannot do it for your children or humanity. There are positive ripple effects on all humankind when you consciously seek spiritual knowledge. But that cannot be your focus or any part of your motivation. You must make this choice with you as the primary beneficiary. All other intentions, noble as they may seem, are simply your mind justifying your efforts. Your intent must be solid, supported by the courage to live truth without engaging mind in guessing what truth is.

The spiritual path is not a part-time study. It cannot be part of your life just when you meditate, or on Sundays, or when you attend spiritual events, and then shelved. If you really want to explore questions that unfold who you are, then a dip in, dip out practice is not enough. Attaining spiritual knowledge is not an intellectual hobby. It is a 24-7 lifestyle, living gently with focus.

This is why an informed choice must be made. Do you want more or do you not? Is the external world with all of its distractions still doing it for you or do you feel that it has an unsavoury emptiness? Are you done with suffering? Is there something inside telling you that there must be more? Is there a yearning within you to find out what it's all about? If you are ready then, make your choice. If not, that is fine: everything has its pace. This is a quest that cannot be forced. It is necessary to make a choice because spiritual knowledge is not theory-based. It is experiential in that realisations and true understanding occur within time and space. It also requires application if you are to yield to this realm within you.

Embracing life with spiritual knowledge brings lightness to your life. It is carefree in nature, open, innocent as a child, gentle, fun loving, easy and liberating. Many have a belief system that says a thing is not worth having unless you work hard for it. If this is a firmly held belief, then this path will be arduous. But note that it does not have to be this way. There are many who find it difficult to receive. These will work hard with their spiritual efforts before rewards are gleaned. If you can allow yourself to have it all (yes to have it all), unconditionally and without cost, then the inner lightness, peace, and calm can be enjoyed as your heart allows, not as your conditioned mind monitors. Take a moment to check within to find out if you are resistant to receiving it all unconditionally. Can you believe this can come to you without hard work or does your belief system say that this is a naive statement? It is your beliefs that will retard the pace of the blessings, grace and joys that are the hallmark of choosing this path.

The age-old idea that spiritual life necessitates denial and sacrifice is a myth. Perhaps it has a place in some religions, but not in spirituality. The concept that causing pain to oneself will earn closeness to God is a fallacy. The merits of sacrifice and denial are gleaned in the area of self-knowledge. They are very useful practises in learning about habits and addictions, and can offer real supports when one wants to break habits that bind, allowing more personal freedom.

On the other hand, discipline is a more useful tool. Having a discipline gives you a framework that enables you to follow guidelines to bring changes to your lifestyle. It gently introduces new habits that allow you to integrate practises in your day. Adopting changes to your life is easier using discipline. There is a belief that discipline runs close to sacrifice, but this is misinformed: they are not connected. Discipline is a gentle practice. It is self-designed so as you can gently nudge yourself towards change. An example of how to apply discipline is in deciding to get up an hour earlier in the morning to make use of that still, clear time of day. A discipline might be to get up four mornings at the earlier time, and to keep your usual schedule for the remaining three. When you work a discipline, there is no negotiation. You are doing this and that is it. The mind agreed to set up the discipline: now the mind must adhere. Following a discipline means that internal, mental negotiation need not happen. In this example, there are days of rest and days of discipline. It balances and brings great rewards in terms of personal achievement and seeing real changes take place in your lifestyle. A carefully-designed, healthy and gentle discipline can reshape your life to support you in how you want to live it.

Perceived ideas of what it means to live a spiritual life can present a resistance to stepping forward. There are many who are concerned about their self-image undergoing change. Some believe that if they embrace change within themselves, they may run a risk of becoming boring socially and vegetarian! Clinging to self-image is a mind game of resistance underpinned by fear of the unknown. On this journey of self-exploration, most discover that as interest in the chatter of mind lessens, an ease and contentment of what is, arises naturally. A consequence of this is a natural fall-off in your interest in taking drugs, alcohol, and eating junk food, coupled with a gladness and ease regarding these changes.

There is evidence to indicate that those who choose this path naturally move towards a more simple living style. They lose interest in the extremes of working obsessively and playing intensively. There is more balance in their approach to life. Lifestyle becomes more natural, more connected to nature and to the earth in many ways. Bright lights and late nights cease to attract their attention. Simpler, calmer, gentle activities mark their lifestyle. These changes take place organically, with habits falling away that are no longer of interest. And so the perception that spirituality produces serious folk or hippies is totally untrue. Many live in total awareness of who they are, silently and discreetly in regular society. This work, if we can call it work, is about enlightenment, not enheavyment!

If you understand and know that seeking spiritual knowledge means paying attention to yourself from the inside, then no outside environment is more conducive than another. It can be useful and a support, but it will never stop you from or encourage you towards progress. Because no matter the daily demands in your life right now, spiritual principles always apply, the truth remains the truth. Your mind can be just as preoccupied sitting on a rock in the countryside as in a crowded supermarket. The focus or work, if you call it that, is within you always.

For centuries, the search for truth was the privilege of those who stepped out of normal life into monastic surroundings to allow themselves the stillness and support to go within. Today, more and more ordinary people like you and I are asking these questions. Monasteries for a few are no longer appropriate supports. Knowledge that was the privilege of the few is becoming widely available. It is time to map routes to enable you to live with spiritual awareness while rearing children, to operate with total inner freedom while holding a job with a value system based in the world that you know holds no meaning for you any more. It is becoming more possible to do this as each year goes by, as spiritual knowledge becomes increasingly available—thanks to the order of things.

You may ask, what then does God have to do with spirituality? The answer is nothing and everything, but this requires expansion. This is an invitation for you to reconsider, take a fresh approach, and re-examine your understanding of what God is. In order to do this, it is necessary to disengage your mind from previously held ideas of God. If we do not take this step, God will be forever an idea that reinvents itself within your limited mind and a great expansion in awareness that awaits you will be postponed again. To explore what or who God is, outside the realms of what we have learned to date, let us first clean out all conditioned thoughts and ideas of what and who God might be.

Religions have presented many images of God through the ages and these served a useful purpose as they suited the awareness of people at that time. God has been depicted as a father, a paternal loving being, creator, a shepherd, a king. God is recorded as being a God of wrath, punishing and rewarding. God is seen as living within the human being, part of who we are, and at other times it was purported that God rests in the inner chambers of the human heart. These images served their purpose at each point in human development. These are models that have been very useful in helping people develop a relationship with God. But all of these are only models and the function of a model is to offer a means to an end. It is not their purpose to offer definition. The human mind cannot define something indefinable and to this end it has been written that God is a mystery.

Within my lifetime, God has moved from being a fearful being in the sky to a loving father who can be a friend. While the images are softening, they are all still simply ideas offering easy identification. They help us develop a certain trust, but through all the centuries these descriptions of God have maintained a sense of separation between humanity and God. A definition of what God is cannot be presented. To do so would be an effort of a finite mind seeking to place limits and labels on that which is beyond mind. Spiritual life takes one to an ever-expanding perspective. To allow this deeper enquiry it is necessary to drop all previously held ideas of what God is. All images and concepts must be set aside to allow yourself a view through a wider lens, a view that is not of your mind but the capacity of a deeper knowing. In the Christian bible it is written that

God is love. Even this will prove limiting as there is that which is beyond even unconditional love.

If you have a belief system that embraces Satan, the devil, as a reality, then it is quite likely that the emotion of fear frequently runs through your feelings. Believing in the devil will develop an ability to act with caution and vigilance. To this end, it serves a purpose in that it teaches one to be awake and aware of what is happening in the present. Fear can motivate you to take a particular action and that can be useful. But as your spiritual awareness grows, you will not need fear to help you choose happiness and freedom. You truly do not need fear to keep you on track. Do you believe you would lose something without this fear? If you were to drop all ideas you have about evil and let a deeper understanding arise within you, there would less judgement within you and fear would begin to subside.

Belief in the devil and in evil, coupled with a capacity to feel deep fear, contributes to their manifestation in your life experience. Having a belief system that embraces evil creates a pigeon hole where acts or events that you do not want to examine closely can be placed in an unsavoury box. Spirituality is about embracing all that is. It does not seek to separate and it does not judge. Drop your belief in your thoughts, images, and ideas, even events that have proven the existence of evil to you. Consider that there is another explanation, but that explanation may not come from your conditioned mind. In order to allow a deeper understanding of all that is, suspend your images, models and convictions of God and Satan.

Most scriptures were written after religions were established; they provide a support system for religion. Taking scripture as literal fact is denying your self-authority and choice to take responsibility for your own life. Some scriptures have served a great purpose in telling people about God and establishing a relationship with God. But for those who are asking deeper questions; scriptures are limited. The answers lie within, no place else. All external influences are limited. They have their use but cannot present ultimate answers. As you become more familiar with listening and trusting your inner feeling and knowing, the practice will take your attention inward to that place of home. All that this book can do is point you inwards, again and again, to let you find the home that you never actually left except in the imaginings of your own thoughts.

Chapter 5
NATURAL STATE

All any adult needs at any time is food, clothing and shelter. Everything else that you might think is required stems from desire. There is never a time when a desire must be fulfilled. This is simply a belief with strong identification that can develop into obsession. If fulfilled desires brought happiness, the world would be a more joyous place for all to live. If you are interested in liberation, then be prepared to drop your desires. However, if you are attached to desires to the extent that you want to realise these self-created goals, then take that path. Spiritual knowledge will not be of interest to you at this time beyond intellectual curiosity.

At all times be honest with yourself. You cannot live out from a level of awareness to which you have not arrived. At a certain time in your evolution, you register the realisation that nothing that the world can give you will satisfy a deep yearning for the truth. Your interest in things of the world falls away naturally. There are some who adopt this position in an intellectual manner: advocating an immunity from pain because of their spiritual beliefs. Invariably life presents them with an uncomfortable lesson in humility and repositions their place in the scheme of things. The inner yearning for truth cannot be faked. There is an inward pull that culminates in the realisation that you are not attached to anything in your life, that you are prepared to walk away from it all and to abandon all desires. However, at this point you also know that there is no other place to go, at least no physical place.

Many have become spiritual seekers. They drift from one esoteric philosophy to another, always looking outside for the missing piece to the puzzle of life or beyond. Many go from healer to shaman to sage, but nothing makes the grade that is required to satisfy an inner longing for spiritual truth. This search is nothing more complicated than a search for your Self. This looking for your Self is a yearning for that feeling of home that yields a complete inner rest and you cannot find it without. The search itself can become a distraction as it motivates activity just like any desire. All searching is driven by thought; even the attaining of enlightenment does not exist beyond a concept. Whatever you do to find your Self will take your attention from it.

Every thought that you ever entertained had its origin in one specific thought. The source of all thought is the thought of "I." The original "I" thought arises and matures to the thought "I AM" and existence is manifest. The very moment "I AM" presents, there exists an idea that burgeons with potential for identification. Identification gives rise to form. As that potential is realised, I am something or someone comes into being. As long as you believe that you are that physical form presented by thought, suffering will ensue: that is the package.

The idea of looking for something, be it a feeling or a state, can only arise when there is dissatisfaction and rejection of what is present. Consider that the desire to be other than you are, to feel differently about yourself or your life, is only a thought distracting you from what is in perfect order, silent and peaceful at a deeper level within you.

Thoughts can distract, give rise to unending desires, and cause sleepless nights. However, there is a sequence to the mechanics of thinking. However chaotic thinking may become, all thoughts arise from one thought: an original movement from emptiness that resonates as "I." All thoughts are equal and powerless. They exist only as imaginings until you choose to give them the weight and power to be true for you. In choosing to believe in your thoughts, you pull them into existence and the drama begins.

Let's take a look to find out what you believe you are. Have you taken it for granted that you are your body? It is easy to recognise that you are not your body (a form). If you were, then in having a limb amputated there would be less of who you are in existence. This is clearly not the case. Even if you lose the more intimate functionings of the body, in the case of your sight or your hearing, you are not less than what you were before. In losing a primary sense, adjustments must be made in your lifestyle and you may have an initial emotional response to these changes in the body. Your level of identification with the body is proportionate to your ability to respond to these new circumstances. Some adjust well to adaptations and some find it more difficult. While adjusting to change is the issue, who you are is never affected. Clearly you are not your body or its functions. If you were, then the same response to permanent changes in the body would be experienced by all.

Are you your thoughts? How could you be your thoughts if you can see that you have them? If you can recognise a thought taking your attention, and then later you are no longer having that thought, then you must have been there also prior to your thoughts. Thoughts come and go. If you can see them how could you be them? There is no difference between mind and thoughts. Mind is simply made up of thoughts and comprises nothing else. When you use your mind, you engage with thoughts. Note also that you have a mind (just as you have a body), and therefore you are not your mind—it is something that you have.

So what or who are you? Peeling back from the world of form and from the world of potential identification, you can place your awareness in the I AM (observer) state of consciousness. From there you can perceive impartially, outside of the level of mind activity that involves identification. In the I AM, in observer mode, you are free from emotional reactions and the flow of what happens prevails with ease. In the I AM state of awareness, things cannot happen to YOU. Things happen and you respond, but that level of identification is not active now. To a certain extent, you are out of the drama and cycle of pleasure, pain and suffering. It is possible to unplug from all identification you hold about yourself. It requires a retraining in thinking, and to this end, this book offers guidelines. Develop the habit of retaining your awareness as the observer of your life. This will yield an enormous freedom, but you will not be able to retain your awareness there permanently, for there is more to be uncovered.

The I AM state is where you are a human being. In the world of form, the tendency is to be a human doing. The fact that you can switch from one modus operandi to another begs the question: who is it that is moving from identification with the I AM formless state to the world of identification with form? Who understands that these two states exist and can grasp the freedom that non-identification offers?

You must be prior to both states. When parents name a baby, they can only do so because they exist prior to the child. If you can recognise the states of both form and formless then you must be there before these also. If you can see from the perspective of your observer then you can also see the observer. Therefore you cannot be your observer either. So who sees the observer? Bring your attention to that which is the ultimate seer. Be there. If you can experience it or if you can talk about it as a phenomenon, then your mind is playing tricks on you. Reject all ideas, images, and experiences. Go to what is seeing the most subtle movement within you.

There will be a direct experience of nothingness, no words, emptiness. There is not even a sense of you. There is no sense of anything. You are That. If your mind now delivers a commentary to you stating that it does not agree that you could be akin to nothingness, that it does not like the image conjured by the term emptiness, then know that the nature of the mind is to doubt. Mind is doing what it does. It's your choice not to believe it. If you are still and remain as That, you will know beyond a shadow of a doubt, beyond the tiniest hesitation, that this is undeniably the truth. This cannot be learned. It can only be discovered to be the truth

truth and that discovery is available to all. This is not a teaching, this is a signpost.

There is no point in reading these words without taking the step to find out who/what is the ultimate seer deep within. If you glide over these words without taking an earnest look within, you are throwing away the most precious diamond that existence can give you. Your natural state is this emptiness and if there is direct experience of this, even the definitions of emptiness and nothingness fall short. Emptiness cannot be it as this word is the opposite of fullness, nothing is the opposite of something and that which you are does not consist of opposites and contrasts. These exist only in the realms of thought.

Why is it so difficult to find words for what you are, for the Ultimate Self? Because words are a product of the mind and the Self is prior and beyond mind. Remove all thoughts, all concepts and there is infinite rest in that which is prior and beyond. Peace is there, silence is there. It has been said that silence is the language of the Self and words are the language of the intellect. Silence is beyond words, beyond mind and communication. Silence in its purest absolute form is Self. It is not that that which is the Absolute is silent, there is nothing to be anything. So that which is, the Absolute, is pure silence. You are That. Hence, Absolute Silence without absence or presence of any kind is your natural state. Abiding in your Self is your natural state. This is the state in which you always are. All that has happened is that your attention has rested elsewhere for quite some time.

Your natural state is not a state of mind: it is not a state at all. But language is limited to such descriptions and to indicate it as a state works well, though it is not a definition. If you cannot go looking for this natural state, then how can it be found? All questions that contain the word "how" come from the thinking, personal mind. You natural state lies beyond your mind. There is no technique to offer, but there are signposts that prove successful for many.

You can experience this: or can you? When abiding in Self there is no you, so in effect you cannot bring yourself there. Neither can you actually experience it as you must shed you to abide there. It may be unfolding to you now that the very subject of you, that which you refer to as yourself, is also an idea: simply a grand collection of thoughts. When this unfolds, it is made known with absolute clarity that all that exists is simply thought.

There is Self and there is thought arising from Self, thought returning to Self and all the while remaining Self. The primary movement is "I." In the beginning, this first came forth from Self, it matured as I AM and then I AM needed an experiencer to experience itself. So the world of form emerged as a physical creation in order to provide an experiencer who could experience an experience. From this we get separation, this and that, wrong and right—the dualistic world as we know it came into being. Perhaps if identification were not so convincing we would not stray so far into this movie created by mind. But we crave experience, we love to feel alive and, even though our interest may lie in living a personal life, the truth of that which you are and cannot, not be, remains the unaffected truth regardless of all.

The beauty of this is that That which you are is beyond time, beyond all thought, so it IS regardless of whatever you are doing or not doing. Abide in the Self, observe from the I AM or plug into the restricting dualistic personal world. Either way, the Self remains unchanged. All arises from the Self, so all is unfolding from that "place" and is returning to that from whence it came. All rivers flow to the sea. Once they merge with the sea, the water that was a river no longer exists as river water. Trying to identify what water in the sea was river water is not possible. It loses that which made it separate, it loses its individuality. River water is not concerned about losing its separateness, it flows towards water and becomes water, yet it always was water. Such is the merging with Self.

From one perspective, there is only one thing that stops you from abiding in the Self: the fear of losing your consciousness of existence. From the world of identification, you lose your current experience of the world and your identity within that realm. So relative or individual existence is pulled like a rug from underneath. But coupled with this, it is revealed that such existence was only a thought, that your identity was nothing more than a conglomerate of self-created and adopted ideas, taken to be true. All your concepts of the world are wiped away like one removes cobwebs from a corner. It becomes crystal clear that all you thought was real was nothing more than all you thought; the reality quality to it was also a thought. As the river loses itself in its merging with the sea, it no longer knows separation and therefore cannot rise to the thought that it was a river. It is at home. It now is the all that is and no thought arises. So, without thought there cannot be an individual who exists apart in any way. To exist apart IS the thought, it is never the reality. Only the Self is real.

Neither can you know the Self, for to know it, you need one to know it and then we have two again, one who knows something that can be known. This presents the triad of a knower, knowing what can be known (knower, knowing and knowledge) and, as you may have guessed, such a triad is only a possibility in the world of form. Self cannot be known. Self is absolute knowledge, not needing to be known and not knowable by any knower. It is absolute, not containing qualities or characteristics because attributes have their opposite. Absolute is Self, Self is absolute. But do not take my word for it. Sit still, be quiet, and don't engage with any thoughts that come: just let them pass without your interest. Do not search for the Self for this would be like your eye trying to see your retina. You are Self, the I AM and you can enjoy form. Your mind can take you to form and the formless I AM. To go beyond the mind simply stop thinking, stop using the instrument that creates the concept of you that you hold onto so dearly. Let mind relax: thoughts will come and go. Do not let your attention cling to any thought in particular. Let go, relax. Without any effort at all, just settle. No doing, no effort.

You will find that you do not arrive in any place. There is only remaining what always was and always will be, outside of time. You are That. Abiding in that, there is nothing to see, feel or know, for feeling, seeing and knowing are functions of the mind. Without mind there is no memory, and so Self is always immediate, new and fresh. There is silence, peace, and no desires. Therefore, there is no sense that this cannot be "it", no feeling arises that there must be more. Absolute totality is present. In becoming familiar with this spiritual knowledge you will see that to say you are this way or like that is unreal, these are concepts only. Identification begins to lose its stickiness if you are willing to release your investment in it. You will see that the mind is not even an entity, rather it is a concept. All that is transient and impermanent is not real beyond the influence of thought. You will see that all of life, the forms and the formless, are nothing more than images reflecting in a mirror, which is Self. The mirror is unaffected and not perturbed by what it reflects. You will see that you are out of it, free from the drama of identification with form and formless. You will see that you never left Self, that you cannot be other than what you are. Only in the imaginings of thoughts that had no real existence did an idea of a person with a life arise for a while. You will see that all that is temporary is unreal, and it will seem totally ridiculous to continue to believe in an undisputable existence of what is transient.

If this unfolds itself as truth to you, and not simply an intellectual exercise, then you are out of it. If this unpacks from a natural aperture, you are out of the drama. Freedom and liberation are limited words, but they point to the direct experience of happiness and joy that arises from this unfolding. A natural acceptance of life unfolds. The harmony and order pertaining to every detail of this physical life is revealed and remains obvious, as if all happens according to common sense. Normal daily living continues and an unshakable inner silence is the power behind each action and word spoken as personal agenda fades out.

Whatever happens to your body or in your life is of no lasting consequence. It is a movie. Instead of being the one citing the script, you can sit as audience. Whatever you have to do to ensure that you (and any dependents) have food, clothes and shelter you will do. Apart from that, the direct experience of bliss for some, joy for others, happiness, peace, and compassion flow through you like an aroma arising from this state. You will ignore the unpleasant sensations. They are part of the play of form also, but they are passing through and do not pull your attention. Only the personal "I" triggers reactive preferences of likes and dislikes. In non-identification, no such judgements take place. There is rest, and the unchanging Self remains unchanged. Nothing attracts your attention because nothing is about you personally. Life continues to happen but, whatever you engage with, there is no longer that density of a personal agenda coming from your part in the play of things.

At this point, consider if what you just read is resonating as the truth within you. If so, re-read this chapter in order to fully gain an intellectual understanding. Then set aside your intellect. There is no need to read anything anymore, simply abide in the Self. Sink into the Self 24-7 until time reveals that time also is a concept and until who is doing the abiding, merges with the Self.

If an inner resonance has not registered this as truth, then watch your intellect with interest. Beware of counter-arguments it presents and know that the doubting mind enjoys control. All your mind can do is present perhaps hard earned beliefs that it will use as resistance to going within. Even the belief that you cannot access the Self is in this category. All these things are activities of mind arising in consciousness, nothing more than reflections from the worlds of form and formless appearing for a fleeting moment on the clear and unperturbed mirror of Absolute.

Chapter 6
DEEP SLEEP

Everybody loves a good night's sleep. Deep, dreamless sleep revitalizes one like nothing else if you can get it! Getting quality sleep contributes to ones whole sense of well-being. Everyone enjoys the experience of deep sleep. So what is so nice about it and why does it feel so good? In addition to physiological benefits, deep sleep offers much more.

When you go to sleep, you go there alone, regardless of who else is in your bed. You must enter sleep alone. In the experience of deep sleep, a dreamless state prevails and effectively there is nothing happening. No world exists, there are no images, the movie is not playing. The perceiving aspect is not present, so no observing takes place. Without a perceiver, there is nothing to perceive. Yet in the total absence of experience, you exist. The "I" with all its beliefs, duties and

responsibilities, the "I" that we cling to in all its importance during the mind active periods, does not exist.
However, in some capacity you are confident that you
do exist in deep sleep. Even if what exists is not the you
that you normally refer to as yourself, it seems that existence is somehow present.

What happens in deep sleep is that all awareness
or consciousness disappears. Consciousness is simply
not present. Consciousness is itself thought or mind,
and to be conscious of anything at all involves mind.
Without consciousness, there is no world, no life, no
family, no work, no laughter, no memory, no emotions,
no past present or future, no right and wrong. The phenomenal world is dependent on consciousness for its
own existence. As long as there is consciousness, the
phenomenal world will continue. However, the world
as you see it with your ideas, labels and opinions of
how it works ceases to exist without your participation
in the conscious state. Investigate further and find out if
this is the truth. Begin by checking out what is permanent and what is impermanent, because you may have
come to know that all that is impermanent is fickle and
transient and is therefore reality in a relative sense only.

Without consciousness, there is no time. Time
itself is a thought. In dropping identification with the
concept of time, it is revealed that there is no world that
continues for you, while you are in deep sleep. The
concept of linear time allows you to experience waking
up some time later as long as you believe in that concept. When the concept of time is still solid, it appears
as a seamless straightforward undisputable sequence of
events that happen in linear time. The belief in time itself ensures this framework. Surprisingly, we do not
seem to have a problem with any of this and we thor-
oughly enjoy deep sleep. Why do we enjoy it so much

when we must go into deep sleep alone and when deep sleep happens without you making it happen? We have no certainty that we will regain consciousness after a period of deep sleep. From past experience we assume we will awaken, yet while in that state we do not care if we regain consciousness. The fear of not coming to in the morning can only exist, like all thoughts, when consciousness is present. There must be one who is willing to believe a fearful thought for it to be experienced. In deep sleep none of this matters.

Why? Because in deep sleep you naturally abide in the Self, or rather there is a natural abidance in the Self. You can know this because there is no perceiver, nobody is there. If there is nobody there and yet you still exist, then you are prior and beyond all thoughts of "I". In deep sleep, you simply drop all that you are not. Your body is resting, but you are not your body. Deep relaxation of the physical body is a consequence of abiding in the Self. It is your natural state, so even your body enjoys it. Abiding in the Self, as experienced directly in deep sleep, facilitates mind rest. There is no thought active, yet you exist and you love it. There is no "I" observing and no experiencing of anything taking place. There is nothing anywhere and no place to call anywhere. There is no "I" thought when the mind is not engaged. Therefore, without an "I", who is the one who would have thoughts? There must be a thinker in order to engage with thoughts. It follows that you can't remember what happens in deep sleep because there is no perceiver either. There is no one to experience it because there is no separation, no identification and therefore nothing to perceive.

When there is nothing to be observed, the observer disappears. There cannot be an observer without material to be observed, just as there cannot be a thinker without thoughts. Both the seer and what is seen, the subject and the object are contents of the mind. In the deep sleep state, the mind falls into abeyance, though existence takes place as always, as Absolute Existence. As the mind is at rest, there is no awareness of the Absolute Self. The Self is there without being consciously experienced. Self itself is not conscious of anything as there is nothing apart from it.

Nothing happens in deep sleep and yet you exist. From this alone you can see that whatever you can gain from any experience does not impact in any way on your existence. You are the silent and unchanging Self, in spite and regardless of all that takes place. What is, the Absolute, never demands and does not require any sensation, any presence, any experience at all to exist. With the absence of mind, in deep sleep there is an absence of the individual. You are Absolute Self and thus the quality of what you are is never dependent on the presence or absence of mind, and is subsequently independent of an individual who is or is not. Similarly, the nature of the Absolute Self is pure knowledge. It does not need someone to know it for it to be knowledge. The Absolute is unaffected, unchanging with or without the triad of a knower knowing what can be known. You are the Absolute and there is thus nothing to be gained or lost. All else is mind.

A residue of the joy and peace that emanates from Self usually lasts for a few moments on coming out of deep sleep, in that momentary space in time before identification resumes its grip. Once mind reactivates, the perceiver resumes its post and very quickly identification ensures that the personal movie begins again. For some, there are just seconds before the gross identification with one's personal story consolidates and poses as reality. As the mind focus moves out to the physical world, ideas of who and what we think we are resume their position within a time and space context. For some, the picture slowly formulates with events, emotions, and responsibilities that surround the leading actor who is yourself. This moment presents an opportunity where you can retain the awareness that the Absolute, the Self, remains unchanged. This is Reality. Instead of letting mind flow outward, retain attention within, in peace and inner rest. You can do this even as your body moves about. Remain with this perception and observe your day unfold from the impartial perceiver viewpoint. All that can emerge in one day is presenting as experiences to be experienced by the personal you. Nothing is actually happening to you unless you want to believe it is. If you do, if identification is present, you will feel the pain and the suffering that goes with a personal life. Daily happenings are nothing more than the transient emergence and subsidence of forms and formless against the unchanging background of the Absolute.

If you identify with the phrase "I want happiness" you can simply remove the "I" that is identification with body and mind and get rid of "want" by dropping desires. What remains? Without "I" and "want" happiness alone remains. It is as simple as this. Similarly, knowledge itself is there prior to there being one to know or not know. Knowledge must be there before all this in order for this "one" to appear. You are That which is prior to one or individuality. You are Absolute Knowledge. To believe, to think and to live out your life as if you were other than Absolute will create pain and pleasure in constant motion, seeking resolution and fulfilment which cannot be found in the realms of creation. Buying into ideas that you are what you think and that your concepts are reality must be totally and unequivocally dropped. The Absolute that you are through it all reveals itself in spite of activity and inactivity of mind. There is a point where you must realise that there is no individual, that you are not "one," that the concept of individuality is a myth.

What you are and cannot not be remains unaffected. This is always the case. That which is present in deep sleep is present right now. This cannot not be present. When you awaken, that which is in deep sleep remains whether you place your attention on it or not. Ironically, there is an action performed by you in taking your attention from that which is Absolute to enable identification with the world of form. To abide in your natural state requires no movement or doing on your part. People ask "what can I do to bring my awareness to the natural state?" The key is in realising that if you didn't do anything, your awareness would not have left it in the first place this morning. Stopping unnecessary mental doing allows the natural state to arise. Deep stillness always rests under an agitated mind.

When you wake up in the morning, consciousness is what awakens, an awareness of mind resumes. You have a body and a mind with which to enjoy experience. At this point, awareness is in the "I AM" and activity can be perceived. Let the perceiving happen. At this moment you do not have to do anything. Notice the tendency to let your mind go out to identify: it is a tendency not a compulsion. Let your mind be focussed inward. Let your attention rest calmly in its natural state. Live your day in the flow that underpins every day: the flow of consciousness. Relax in the knowledge that there is a natural state that you may consciously return and sink your attention into during the day when you observe that you are operating under the laws of identification. This is not a task. If you try to achieve this and set it up as a goal, your mind is involved and you will log jam at the outset. Relax. Resting mind activity disarms gross identification. There is no "how" to stop thinking. Simply stop getting involved in the stories of your thoughts. Stopping is not a doing, not a technique, not to be learned. Neither is it a big deal. Just be quiet, be still, and stop participating in the imaginary world created by your thoughts. There is no identification when the mind is not engaged with thoughts; no suffering is a consequence of no identification.

Meditation in the early morning hours can assist in keeping the mind focused inward. For many, this helps sustain your attention on remaining the perceiver of all activities for much of the day. In breaking the habit of gross identification, meditation is a most useful tool. It trains the mind to become singularly focused and keeps attention inward. Meditation in the morning curbs the habit of outward identification and can build an awareness and familiarity in consciousness of the I AM state. Once identification is active, once you believe that the activities in your day are happening to a personal you and affecting you, your mind is subjectively processing new material and is building more memory, more stories, more ego. The choice is yours.

While spiritual practices like meditation have their benefits, it is best to participate in practices to which you are naturally drawn. In this way, the play of consciousness is leading you to experiences; this is the natural unfolding of your life. To participate in spiritual activities because it's a good idea and because others said it is right for you or because you want a particular outcome creates arduous activity that you will abandon sooner or later. What is for you cannot pass you by. Let yourself be moved, or not, towards spiritual practices in a gentle and natural way, and you will have an innate openness to all it presents.

Your mind plays many tricks on you. Its subtleties must be recognised for you to gain objectivity regarding such tricks. An effective trap is the thought that you will be better off when... you have more routine in your life, when the kids are reared, when you lose weight, when you are fit, when you have savings set aside, when you retire, when you can keep your New Year's resolutions all through the year! The trap is the phrase "I will be better off when..." Your mind does not discriminate what will make you better off; anything will do as your conditioning will complete the statement with personally convincing beliefs. Consider that this is as good as it gets. Here now is how it always will be, no rose tinted make-believe future can alter the truth. Your capacity to be happy does not improve when certain conditions are in place. That is just a thought. There are no circumstances that can give you lasting happiness. Right now, remove that thought, be quiet, sit still and rest in the I AM, as observer. All your beliefs and desires are happenings in consciousness. Let them pass: there is no need to make them yours. Nothing is needed at all right now. With certainty you can know that all is well and it cannot be any other way. Situations come and go. Invariably, if you invest in any thought at all, it will bring suffering. Deep sleep appears to be a much safer option! This stillness is available to you now. Without editing your thoughts you can know that every thought that you entertain as yours is all that distracts you from enjoying deep silence within. Rest in the observing I AM and allow your awareness to sink into That which is seeing even the observer.

In the waking state, the mind is terrified of the idea of emptiness, of vastness. In deep sleep, what is beyond emptiness and vastness is experienced directly and all is found to be exquisitely fine. But mind seeks limitations. It likes to play safely, to be in control and manage things. Your natural state is to be at peace, but mind only knows peace as a concept so it will try to create peace for you. It can even make peace a practice to keep you attached to the realms of ideas and personal beliefs. As you learn to observe with no attachment, peace arises. The only thing that can attempt to interfere with this is your identification with thoughts.

Training the mind to be still is of great benefit, but it yields a state of mind like so many other states. Stillness of mind is an experience to be enjoyed. This kind of stillness is not what you are: this stillness is a concept and a valid experience and is relative. If something can be experienced it can only exist relatively. It is not the truth. All experiences come and go. Truth remains, unchanging and complete. Do not stop short on your inner enquiry just because your mind is still. If you can experience stillness, you will also experience agitation. All states have their opposite. Do not decide that stillness or an experience of peace is enough. There is no experience that can give you anything other than experience. Reject all such tricks that the mind presents. In sinking into that which is prior and beyond all thoughts, all states of mind, all experiences, resting in the beingness that sees but cannot be seen, it is revealed that beyond the shadow of a doubt mind itself does not exist. Mind is only a concept.

At the end of the day, you will reach a point of knowing that there is nothing to learn and nothing to experience. However, there is something that makes itself known to you, and in that realisation there begins a slow loosening of the habit that has you pretending to be what you are not. Mind may even put this point on a checklist: if this realisation has not happened to me, I cannot experience what I really am. This too is thought. Whatever your experience is of what you are, this is but a playful unfolding taking place within the totality of what you really are. No matter how gross the identification with thought, this too is an expression of Self through form. It is all Self. It cannot not be. Any ideas you have about this material are from your mind. Mind can fake it up to a point; it constructs the most subtle experiences. Do not stop at experiences and do not stop with any conclusion. Know that all concepts come from mind. Stay in neutral gear, no stickiness of any sort, free flow without an objective, remain totally open and watch without expectation. Whatever appears in time and space cannot last. As you remain unattached the core essence that is you, within your beingness will come forward and will begin to unfold exquisitely. Expect this to take place and rest assured it never will. Engage a commentary from mind and it all stops again. Once you identify with a thought, any thought, the core essence of what you are yields to your chosen distractions. Absolute Self needs nothing to be what it is. It is not bothered whether you continue to believe in separation or not. All is unfolding from Self. Nothing can stray away from Self or lose Self. These are thoughts too. All is contained within Self.

The moment you think you have spiritual knowledge or that you know how it works, identity is present, mind is active, and further identification is taking place. How does one know when mind is involved? Simply because the mental capacity always has a personal agenda. With real discovery, Silence is beyond description, the personal "I" is nowhere, nothing can be said, there is nothing to be said. Draw no conclusions, keep quiet and observe. That which IS cannot be an idea. It manifests all that is formless and all that has form. It enjoys activity and actually plays through these manifestations. It is not contained or held by anything it has manifested. It is the ultimate and is the essence of you. Confusion arises in the realm of mind only, but even this is transient as it too is part of the play.

Chapter 7
THERAPY

With the turn of the century, there is an unending supply of new therapies coming on stream in western urban communities. Are we really so broken that we must be healed? Are we so dirty that we need to be cleared and cleansed? Are these not simply thoughts also or is there a genuine validity to the healing industry?

Everything in existence is valid: from a stone to a war zone everything has its place. What can be delivered is entirely another matter. Creation presents an option for you to engage with all that is available to you, simply to have experiences in every which way that they can be had. There is no quality-control inbuilt in creation. All is for you to judge if you choose to do so. Reject or accept what is offered and this makes no difference to creation. It is just one unfolding action: becoming form in every way possible and returning to its source at its own pace. Your body and mind are part of this, experiencing change and instability on a base within you that is beyond time, beyond what can and cannot be, in complete unchanging rest.

All therapies, personal development, and what are sometimes called new age techniques, are part of this manifestation. Can they deliver on the promise of transformation? If your mind identifies with transformation as something you want, desire is active and you may or may not have this experience. But one thing is for certain, all results no matter how revolutionary at the time, will be temporary because all therapeutic work takes place in the realm of mind; using mind to resolve mind, replacing one concept with another. What mind deems as undesirable thoughts are generally replaced with more pleasant ones. Therapy cannot go deeper than this as all personal experience is still within the realm of the personal "I." Mind cannot and will not lead you out of mind. Even the esoteric, angelic work, wisdom from Atlantis and shamanism, is all mind. Such work makes most sense when one believes in separation: that there is you and another. Every path is a legitimate path offering what can be fantastic experiences and a wonderful sense of liberation that lasts for a while. Only the ego can reap these benefits. If you are open, therapeutic work helps refine the ego, making you more pliable and open to shifts in perspective and helping you move outside rigid beliefs. To this end, it serves a wonderful purpose. Engage in that to which you are naturally drawn. Proceed towards what makes sense to you and, in time, the attractions towards therapy will fall away of their own accord.

To take up the idea that there is something you need to do and a destination for you to arrive at will serve to create a seeker within you. It establishes a belief system that you must do something to be something or someone that you are not already. All of this is thought. It is nothing more solid than conditioned thinking playing out. As long as the idea that you have something to gain holds credibility for you, then you will seek. Seeking is valid, but it cannot lead you to the treasure of your deepest yearning. All searches are ultimately for the Self, for the home within. While there are many levels of seeking, they all culminate at a point where the activity of searching is recognised as the outcome of a habitual thought and thus seeking ends. One discovers that what you are looking for is precisely where you are looking from. As you abide in the Self and identification with thoughts is lessening, your experience will be that whatever needs to be refined within you will be automatically realigned. This happens by itself without effort by you or interference from you. In this way consciousness takes care of itself.

Therapies may deepen your understanding of your conditioning, your emotions, etc. However, as long as you continue to identify with thoughts then, as you unravel in therapy, you will quickly create more drama if your habit of identifying with thoughts remains. In any moment, you are either observing effortlessly or you are believing your thoughts. Therapy is a path that can be taken like any other but, if you think it will fix you, you may be better served to examine whether there is truth in the belief that you need to be fixed. Also, if you want something out of therapy, what you will get from that desire can only yield a temporary satisfaction. To want something leads to suffering because, at the outset, you think you are missing something. If and when you get it, it cannot last. Wanting is suffering. Not wanting is the natural state. Therapies can show you your patterns of thinking. Skills can be learned to help you better engage with life. If this interests you, self-enquiry is not of interest to you. Engaging with life experientially has a stronger pull than the search for truth. Know that the mind will disguise the former as the latter effectively. Both yearnings cannot happen within you at the same time.

There is a place for everything: a place for every therapy within the order of all that can be manifested. If you believe you are not ready for self-enquiry yet, that too is your experience unfolding from your thoughts. If inner enquiry attracts you, if it creates an excitement within you, then let that alone lead you. If spiritual practice draws your attention and has a rightness to it, then take that path. If therapeutic support, in any methodology, has a feeling of rightness to it, embark on that route with openness and honesty.

Consciousness will find its own practice until it becomes more appealing to ask yourself who is it that is practising. Then, honing down the ego falls from your interest, reshaping inner qualities ceases to make sense as a worthwhile methodology, and the burning question to find out what or who you are becomes central. It is then that you are knocking on the door of the Absolute Self. All ideas about things that will help you are thoughts arising from the mind. You can choose to believe them into existence or not. It is wise to drop any judgements you may have about levels of consciousness being high or low, one being more evolved than another. All of that is mind and total rubbish. There is but one play of consciousness. The belief that individual souls share this planet will dissolve as an illusionary concept as you come to know with absolute certainty that a personal "I" does not exist beyond your own mind. Remember that you see the world as you are, not how it really is.

Abiding in the Self is not the reward for working through a process. There is nothing to work through. In fact, no amount of energetic, emotional or mental processing will result in realising the Self. Equally, no amount of spiritual practice will directly result in self-realisation. These are simply thoughts arising in consciousness. Consciousness is not concerned with working things out; it does not seek resolution. Nothing needs resolution. All unfolds as it unfolds. Everything that can possibly be, that you can perceive as an object, a project, a methodology, a technique, be it physical or in thought, is arising in consciousness. It will subside and have its death in consciousness. All is changeable in consciousness. There is nothing else. Literally there is no-thing else. What you are is beyond things, beyond states, forms, and non-physical forms. You are what is and that is unchanging. Consciousness is simply mind watching what has come from mind and it is all a thing of nothing.

If you do not limit yourself to being an individual, a whole package of stories will disappear with that limitation. As you recognise your capacity to observe without identification, an automatic inner tidying up of erroneous beliefs begins to take place. If there is an inner recognition of this taking place for you, then fear and anxiety vanishes. Everything settles by itself into a perfect emptiness. No turbulence remains and it cannot feature until you pick up your next thought.

It increasingly becomes evident that nothing matters. Bothering with your conditioned thoughts is recognised as pointless. Tendencies can be in your body, but are they you? What arises in the body will fade and what arises in the mind also fades. Pay no attention to what is presented by mind. You are not that and it is not your concern. If your mind tells you to pay attention to the observer and remain as the Self, then that is a thought. Simply be what you are. There are no "shoulds" in self-enquiry. When you fully understand that which you are and cannot not be, there is nothing to do to be what you are. In the beginning, some action takes place. You need to remind yourself not to identify with thoughts. There is a habit to be broken. You will be drawn to breaking it and it will break. In time, the unfolding of consciousness dissolves the magnetic pull to identify with thoughts, and then ever increasingly thoughts will pass by without your personal interest.

Let thoughts and feelings come, let shock flow through you, let physical pain come. Observer does not have the capacity to like or dislike whatever manifests, only mind has these concerns. The observer does not want the pleasant moments to stay and unpleasant feelings to go quickly. It has no investment in either, it is impartial. What is good and bad can only be recognised qualitatively by your mind. When these judgements take place as likes and dislikes, you know you are not viewing as observer. Observe all that changes, you do not change. There is no need to interfere in any way. Do not be concerned with the opinions of the ever changeable and conditioned mind. Do not let any thought of what is pleasant or unpleasant be yours. Everything that is temporary changes of its own accord—this is the perfect order of things. In seeing this, a great burden is removed, such is the experience if you realise this to be so. There is a wonderful helplessness to be enjoyed as it is revealed that what is good and bad, nice and ugly are in fact not so, beyond your thoughts. Things simply are. All qualitative commentary comes from the conditioned mind.

Then it makes no sense to take criticism or praise personally; likes and dislikes are thoughts and have nothing to do with what you are. Every thought and every opinion that can exist will exist at some point. None of this belongs to you. In fact, if you follow these steps at a level deeper than your intellect, you will see that personal in any context is a concept that holds no weight for you. A force that is not from a sense of personal action takes care of all that must be done during your day, sometimes moving through your form and sometimes not. Drop identified thoughts and let it happen naturally. Sink into the simplicity of I AM. Let this stand alone without a concept to define your personality. All definitions, other than I AM were picked up during your life and should a desire to define yourself arise, do not go there. It is the tendency of the ego to grab hold of something, a value, a story, an opinion, that it can use to reconsolidate an identity for you. You may see that every single thought you can entertain only serves to perpetuate the personal "I." The most subtle of all thoughts is the concept of "I" and from there ego is born. Without the "I", you will clearly see that you are not the creator of your feelings or your thoughts. Thoughts simply pass by like clouds moving across the sky of consciousness. If you identify with either passing thoughts or feelings, you will give them life force and an egoic state resumes for you. Feelings and thoughts flow through you, that is life. They cannot bother you in any way without your identification with them.

If you remain in observation of all that passes through, you will come to recognise that you are not even observing. You will see that the action of observation effortlessly flows through your physical form. Observing is not something to do; that is simply an idea, a concept. Observing itself is a concept also. The power that plays in every conceivable way through physical form is Absolute Silence. The formless I AM enjoying and perceiving may appear as a limited perspective. Know that this resistance is from mind. All resistance, once seen for what it is, passes quickly. Resting in I AM is a natural thoughtless state. A silence arises within as thought is absent and deep joy is present. This silence does not offer a life force to engage with gossip or idle chatter; it does not find words to tell stories of insignificant experiences and opinions that even most subtly serve to reinforce a personal "I." Inner peace and a natural calm prevail. All appears as normal on the outside but within you are empty, happy and silent.

There is a hopelessness and a helplessness that brims with relief and lightness in the realisation that it is totally pointless to push against the flow of what is the harmonious order of the universe. From the silence of no mind, that flow is visible and observable, and so all motivated effort is recognised as futile and superfluous to what has already been addressed.

Chapter 8
SELF-ENQUIRY

Self-enquiry simply means to enquire into yourself to find out what or who you are by placing investigative attention within. When undertaken correctly, there is direct experience of the natural state, of the Self. Self-enquiry is intellectual in the beginning, because there is a partial technique that needs to be understood. At the outset of self-enquiry, it is necessary to make an effort to abide in the Self. This results in a natural abiding in time. The unnatural state of an outward focused mind must be brought around to being inward focused, and this alone is where effort lies. Mind thinks it has something to do in order to realise its true nature. It only has to be quiet, not engage with thought and then it must be bypassed. Because mind is a reflection of the Self, it is entirely dependent on the

Self. This must first be understood and then realised to be so.

An explanation of self-enquiry is full of paradoxes. This cannot be avoided as long as one uses language to go beyond the mind. The finite can describe the infinite but, beyond the infinite, the mind becomes redundant in the process and ceases to exist. This happens in spite of the mind, because the mind cannot go beyond existence. It seeks experiences to validate existence. Its purpose is to perpetuate existence so it will not and cannot willingly surrender to its own annihilation. Mind will want to come with you in self-enquiry and will attempt to do so initially. To this end mind is likely to set up a checklist of what to do, what to feel, how to experience and what to expect. It will assess how you are doing and compartmentalise self-enquiry as a spiritual experience culminating findings as interesting phenomena. While enquiring within, if you see light or colours—reject them. They are concepts. If you meet angelic beings or spirit guides—reject them. The tricks of the mind are many. The Absolute contains no manifestations, no concepts or images, no "I" and no other. To have an experience of any sort is your imagination at play. This is not self-enquiry; this is mind doing what mind does. Mind perceives that which is beyond I AM as a void, blank and stagnant because mind cannot go beyond phenomena. In self-enquiry, if you think that you understand it, that you got there, that you found the holy grail, that you know how to do it, then you have not touched anything beyond mind. You have delved deeper into the creativity of your own imagination. Even the desire to realise the Self will ensure your attention stays in the realm of mind. Self-discovery and inner questioning of this ilk is interpreted by the mind as another opportunity to engage an experiencer in experiencing an experience. Self-enquiry is not and cannot be an experience. Self can only be intuited in the absence of mind. Expect mind to vehemently reject this, as it will not want to face the fact that its very presence is the greatest impediment to performing this enquiry.

Self-enquiry is so simple and easy that we can miss it. There is such praise for effort in society that to make no effort can initially be puzzling. Many schools of spiritual thought purport that humanity has a long way to go to reach a resolution or satisfactory evolution. This is rarely questioned. It is accepted as truth and is believed into existence. There is no journey and the idea that evolution can take lifetimes is untrue. If you believe you have a lot of work to do to transform yourself—that you will find your authentic self at the end of your dysfunctional marriage, your anxiety or your grief—this is not so. You are the witness of all of this. But if you want to believe that you have a distance to travel, then you will find places to go to, books to read, seminars and courses to attend and a journey to take.

The "I" thought is the source of all thoughts because you cannot have a thought without a thinker. All thoughts arise in consciousness and your mind has you believing that the thoughts you entertain are actually yours. All of your thoughts are in relation to you: your opinions, your life, your hopes, your dreams, your career, your ideas and beliefs. Identification cannot happen without the sense of "me" and "mine." In truth there is no yours and mine. Thoughts are thoughts, but you can make thoughts your own by turning on the personal and subjective perspective that is ego. This happens, for example, when you think you will be better off without thoughts. Wanting to control thinking is it-

Born to be Free

self a thought. Even in observing thoughts, if you have a preference not to be attached over being attached to thoughts, then this too is mind. One can be firmly attached to the idea of not being attached! To have a preference of any kind is mind. In order to believe the story your thoughts present, you must at some level want to own your thoughts. Thus you consolidate the idea that there is a thinker who needs these thoughts. Hence, every thought has its origin in the "I" thought. Self-enquiry directs one to the source of this "I" thought.

Be quiet, sit still, do not participate in any thoughts, leave mind activity aside for now and direct your attention to the source of the "I" thought. The "I" thought is the original personal thought and it is therefore mind itself. Placing your attention on the source of the "I" thought leads to something within you that is behind, prior to or beyond the mind. Ask the question "From where does the I thought arise?" It is the source of all thoughts and, in trying to locate the source of the most intimate thought of "I" you will find that it is no more than a concept. The source of all thought has no separate existence: a sense of nothingness leads you to Pure Self.

Ask the question "Who is having this original I thought?" In words of Bhagavan Sri Ramana Maharshi (1879-1950) ask within, "Who am I?" From where did this question arise? Look within and find out from where did the "I" arise. This question turns your vision around. When you solve this for yourself and confirm your findings with absolute clarity, you have solved all other conceivable questions. There is no answer to either of these questions. To arrive at any describable answer would be a conceptual response from your mind. Stop reading and settle within right now. You are capa-

84

ble of this enquiry this very moment. Go within and prove it to yourself. See if you can locate the source of the thought of "I" or ask, "Who am I?" See what you find.

It takes common sense to know that you cannot point to anything, be it object or image, and claim that you are that. If you see an object, you are at a distance from it—so it is not you. Therefore, you must be more subtle than that. In this search or enquiry, find that which you refer to as "me." For a long time, you have accepted that "me" to be real, so locate it now. Focus your attention and see if this one, whom you refer to as "me", can be found. Do not make this complicated: it is simple. Initially, there will be resistance to this inner search, as many aspects of personality do not want to discover truth. Do not give up and do not accept a conceptual answer. If a thought arises as your thought, know that it cannot exist without the presence of your ego or personal "I." Recognise what is at play and let thoughts pass by. Do not entertain them as real. When there is the "I" thought, you, he, and she all appear as separate entities. See if the "I" thought refers to a tangible entity. Apart from a subject in thought, does this "I" exist? If this enquiry is undertaken correctly, you will see that all your ideas and beliefs about others are not tangible entities. They are nothing but concepts. All are the same in essence and different in expression, nothing more. If you let the "I" thought dissolve, then all differences must (and will) disappear.

This discovery is not an academic or intellectual exercise. If you just learn about it, all is lost to you. Discover for yourself that whatever you observe, you cannot be. So stay as witness and let all come and go. You will find that a peace arises, settling your attention in a restful way. Observing is effortless. Look to see what are you, where are you, who are you, and you will find that there is no tangible, identifiable thing of substance that is you. Neither is there a location where you can be found. You will discover that it is only your conditioning that says that this "I" is real. The "me" that resists, feels separate, and has a story is a thought. Neither that "me" or mind has any more substance than any thought, all are thoughts. Personality itself is only an idea existing within you. None of these things are tangible, none of these are real. See them as a play within creation. There is no "I," there is no "me" and all that is "mine" is a derivation of these concepts. You are emptiness. Give no identity or label to this direct experience. There is seeing taking place, but there is no "you" engaged in the activity of seeing. Remain indefinable. There is no need to engage with anything that arises. Even fears that you will explode, combust or disappear may vie for attention. Do not engage in any thought at all now. What explodes, combusts or disappears cannot be you. A natural sense of peace and wellness arises from this discovery.

Being empty in this way is completely natural. This natural state does not need protecting. You are the peace you are searching for and there are no conditions. You will find that mind itself slips into this infinite peace naturally. Engage in this wonderful discovery for yourself right now, as all this book can do is present concepts to indicate truth—it cannot present you to you. Do not identify with mind that is full of doubts stating, "I am not there yet" or "I will just read to the end and then do the self-enquiry." Do not reach for an experience. There is no event to take place. Ultimate understanding is present and it is empty.

Of all thoughts that can be thought, the "I" thought is the root. Mind is thus nothing other than the "I" thought, and so mind and ego are the same thing. It follows that the individual "I" is nothing but ego. Every time you speak a sentence that begins "I am ...." you endorse a belief that you exist. Identifying yourself as an individual perpetuates you as an object. But you are the subject and there is only the subject. If you believe there is an independent you who exists as a separate entity, then enquire as to what and who exactly it is that exists. Find out who is this "I" that you refer to as yourself. You will find that, in removing this primary thought, all other thoughts and concepts are loosened and can be uprooted. What remains then? Pure Self. This is not consciously experienced because no objective centre is found. No form is located, yet somehow there is intuitive emptiness. Coupled with this recognition immense joy and peace arises. You cannot be what you can point to or experience. You are the primary, the Self. This reveals itself beautifully from stillness with absolute clarity. Prove inwardly that you are the Self, beyond a shadow of a doubt. Thoughts can arise, but significance will not be present. This is because the one who is interested in thoughts, to whom all concepts impact, is simply not here. In this natural state beyond mind, what once was a sticky relationship with thought is now broken.

In the dropping and destruction of all "I" thoughts, self-enquiry must also destroy itself. In dissolving an "I", there is no longer one to ask this very question of self-enquiry. Hence, there cannot be an answer to the question. You are the answer to the question: not an individual, conceptual "you", but who you really are beyond concepts, thoughts, ideas and whatever mind creates. Self-enquiry brings on the death of the personal "I." In asking "Who am I?", there is silence with no answer. To arrive at an answer denotes mental exercise. With no mind, there is no doubt; there is profound silence. There is no you that can claim it, hold it, describe it, have an insight into it. You cannot even remember it and there is no memory to be visited within it. Memories are only needed by ego in order to play with identification. It happens in reference to a past and a future. In the Self, there is no need for such impressions or for anything to register. These are functions of mind. Thus, no one can claim to know it, for in the Self there is no one. It is impossible to register it as an experience, as mind is the necessary backdrop to experience. To make such a claim requires one. With the rise of the concept of one, separation comes into form and we are in the world of mind again. We are telling a story of one who had an experience. That is not the direct experience of Self—that is mind.

Ask the question "Who am I?" This useful signpost is effective for many. Drop the signpost once it is used. Holding onto the question is mind seeking control. Ask the question and let the rest reveal itself to you. Let the question dissolve and let the questioner dissolve. What remains is what you are. Effortless and Absolute. Self-enquiry will pull you from the drama that arises from identification with thoughts every time. If you initially self-enquire at every opportunity, asking "Who am I?" or "Who is angry?" or "Who is waiting for this bus?" or "Who is it that is annoyed by that comment?" or "Who is suffering this pain?", this will help you step from the drama of your own conditioning to observe and then beyond, to Reality. With such intensive practice, self-enquiry becomes exhausting, but from this point on you will begin to find a way and a pace appropriate for you. Consciousness will ensure that a balance is found. Let the question "Who am I?" take a strong hold on you so that you cannot think of other thoughts. This questioning is not to be taken lightly. It requires active looking with your full attention. Check inwardly and constantly ask, "What is the sense of "I" attached to now?" See the concept or the intention and observe. Do not identify. It will become obvious that what you are observing is a movement in the space of consciousness—and you are not that. Know that you cannot have spiritual knowledge without diverting and dissolving attention through self-enquiry. Mental effort is not enough. It must be directly experienced to come to the certainty of the true nature of what arises as "I." When this is inwardly understood, the annihilation of the questioner comes. Self-enquiry will be a mental activity at first. Be aware of this and work through this phase. The certainty that you are the Absolute consolidates. Ego increasingly subsides and thoughts lose their identification potency. With self-enquiry, there occurs a natural thinning and dissipation of old habits, patterns of thinking and obsessions, and with continued enquiry you will cease to create new mental distractions. Each time you revert to Self, there is freshness to that eternal freedom and space that you are.

The idea that you are separate in any way arises only from your mind. When you seek to find the real nature of mind, you will discover that there is no mind. When you abide in Self, mind is nowhere. Therefore to be concerned about that which is only a thought is totally pointless. Once the mind accepts the fact that it has no power of its own, but is enabled to function by a higher power called Self, it will yield and dissolve in Self. All that is involved is a subtle movement of attention to examine where in you does the thought "I" originate.

There is no bridge to the Self because there is no gap between the Self and anything else that can exist. You are the Self. Believing that you are otherwise brings suffering and pain. There is no place to go and nothing to do to make you more of what you already are. How you experience yourself is up to you. To make self-enquiry another spiritual exercise creates another habit of mind. It is best to relax, stay quiet and stop engaging with thoughts. All unfolds naturally, revealing the truth by a power that takes care of all arising in consciousness, together with consciousness itself. All things come and go—let them. That within which all things come and go is unaffected. Remove your attention from all that is transient. That which remains never came from anywhere. It cannot be experienced by a second. It is Absolute Self.

With the direct experience of Self, is it viable to play small and identify with the petty stories of likes and dislikes, desires and judgements of your personal mind? Concepts are part of all that is. They are part of consciousness and entertaining them as truth creates difficulties. In the inevitable dropping of every concept you have about yourself, you will find that the most rigid of beliefs is the belief that you are your body. Drop everything and rest in what you are. Phrases such as "I am that I am" or "I am not that" can be useful, but they will not point your attention to Self. For most who undertake self-enquiry, the question "Who am I?" directs one to a wonderful treasure. Finding the source of the primary thought—the "I" thought—reveals the core. Self-enquiry is not a process or a practice. There are no steps. It cannot take you some place. It simply points you in a direction that enables you to look and see from where the question "Who am "I?" arises. Without thinking, without effort, the root of your mind is challenged.

In the absence of any concept of what you are and are not, Self is. That which says "I" in you is found to be nothing more than a thought itself. You are prior to this original thought of "I." Find out who is watching this "I" and who is the Ultimate Seer of that? When you can observe something or point to something, it is clear that that cannot be you. So, to that end, you cannot observe the Self either. There is no recognising the Self. Experience it directly. To abide in the Self is a signpost to be used and discarded, because nobody can abide in it. You cannot stay in it. How can you stay in what you are? You are what you are. Exactly what that is awaits your discovery again and again. When there is direct experience, there is no you experiencing, only the experience is, in pure form. So you cannot stay in it, and it follows that you just have to be it. This is what the phrase "abiding in the Self" points towards. You cannot become it. It is already what you are and Self can never become more or less of what it is. So, be what you are, for there is no "how" question to any of this. "How" always stems from mind. The Self cannot know Self: it is even beyond oneness, and oneness is said to be beyond separation and unity. Self can only be Self, and so be what you cannot not be. To be what you are is totally fulfilling. It is not that you, as a person, can feel fulfilled, but Absolute fulfilment arises in the transcending of all ideas of who you thought you were. It is not that you shift identity from being an individual to Absolute. Look and see for yourself. There is only Absolute and your imagination. Which are you in your essence? Satisfaction that arises from the Self is so complete that there is no interest in anything else, in anything phenomenal. There is no dependency on your body, your life events or on anything that can be experienced. This is because no individual "I" exists who needs to be fulfilled. What you are is happiness, total, complete, freedom beyond the concept of freedom. The physical body becomes totally relaxed, enjoying a great ease that flows as a consequence of abiding in your natural state.

If this resonates as truth for you, if these signposts lead you to that which you are, then where lies the purpose in spiritual healing or religion? If you are in the grip of believing thoughts about being broken, about needing to be healed, fixed, understood, witnessed, are these not thoughts laden with identification? Does it serve you to continue such gross identification? Any experience that life can present to you, beyond the event of experiencing, can only become a thought in a past that does not exist. Dissolving it, letting it go, cutting the ties with it are all simply concepts within consciousness and have nothing to do with spiritual knowledge. The healing industry, angels and chakra work, churches, religions and rituals are not routes that lead to truth. They offer experiences only. All that exists is part of the play of the activity within consciousness, bringing experiences to those who seek experiences. Spiritual and therapeutic work can help in shifting limited thinking about how things work. It can only replace one set of thoughts for another. Spiritual knowledge is instantly attainable. There is no money to be spent, no place to go, no standards to reach. In spite of all these mind constructs, experiences and happenings in consciousness, the Self remains unchanged. All experiences exist solely for your enjoyment.

The traditional order of evolution of mind from spirituality to deeper questioning begins with focusing on an external object such as an image of God/guru or repeating a mantra. All the while, a dualistic perspective prevails. There is a subject and an object. Therefore a relationship between both necessitates a belief in separation. However, this is a useful methodology to train the mind to be singularly focused. When concentrating on one thought, all others disappear. As this honing down of mind takes place, simultaneously you will find yourself gradually withdrawing from external objects in all aspects of life, with the realisation that nothing external satisfies and attention stays on the subject. Finding out who the subject is, who this "I" is, becomes central. Desires are understood as the play of mind. Questioning from where does this "I" notion arise, and in the subsequent merging with what is found, it is revealed that there is only the subject. There is no second, no object, and this resonates as truth even beyond the concepts of subject and object. Thus, it becomes clear that to consider God as something external to oneself is a mental image, a mere play of mind.

As long as God is personal, that personal God must be external to oneself—a personal God is believed into existence by a personal mind. As long as you believe you are your body, you will perceive others independently exist as their presenting forms. Similarly, if God is a form for you, you must first believe that you are a form. Beyond identifying mind and thus beyond form, the essence of all is the same. Thus, an image of God is no different from God when you realise that form is not synonymous with essence. Hence, there is divinity and sacredness in every single thing, manifest and unmanifest, all is the same in essence and different in expression. Absolute Divinity is Self: it is without name and form. Do not be under the impression that the Self can be a personal God. Self is Absolute; it is nameless, formless, divinity. It is the reality from which everything arises and into which all will merge again. Even a personal God, saint, or guru who appears for you as real from time to time emerges in consciousness from the nameless and formless. Appearance as form is dependent on consciousness. Ultimately, all forms return to Self from whence they came and the Absolute depends on nothing.

So what will bring you to happiness? Temporary experiences of happiness may be familiar to you, but at a certain point that is not good enough. If you want to feel happy then ask, "Who is the one who wants to feel happy?" It is the mind that desires happiness, and it is the mind that wants to feel the Absolute, to rest in Absolute Peace and Joy. But how can mind feel that which is permanent? Permanent Presence can be felt directly once the mind is quiet. It is not difficult to put aside your mind once it is quietly relaxed. Once attention is available, that which is permanent will reveal itself, because there isn't any "one" to interrupt. It is only mind that interrupts the spontaneous current of the Self. Similarly, know that peace that can be disturbed by a thought is not Absolute Peace. Mind cannot bring you to the direct knowledge of Self. The Absolute remains unaffected by all that comes and goes, and is constant and indifferent to all conditions.

If there were conclusive signposts to the Self, surely this would be well known information. Consciousness has been unfolding since the beginning of time. Its coming into existence created time and space as a context. Consciousness is not bothered by what unfolds as form or as formless. It has no concern for, or judgements about, anything: it functions to accommodate the existence of everything that can be created, everything and its opposite. Every thought that can be conceived takes place in consciousness. All the while consciousness itself is not affected. Consciousness is not in a hurry to draw creation towards a resolution. Its nature is to enquire into itself, but there is no conclusion, no answer that can satisfy in consciousness. Consciousness will never work itself out, for that is impossible. It is your option to simply get off the roundabout once you come to understand and know the truth of this game of consciousness, the leela or play of creation.

Consciousness arises from the Self and is at no time not Self. Anything that is identifiable, is an appearance in it. All that has form is a unique expression of essential essence that is Self. So how can there be a returning home, a reconnection back to source or God? All such ideas are concepts. It is only from your mind that the idea that you are separate in any way can arise. Any sense of separation is a construct emanating from the "I" thought. Any experience of separation is untrue and based on learned, conditioned beliefs. There is a natural order to the flow of consciousness at all times. Everything unfolds in its own time. Do whatever you feel inwardly drawn to do. Do nothing if you are drawn to inactivity. After all, you literally only need food, shelter and clothing. The unfolding of experience will continue: know the truth, remind yourself of it if you must, and enjoy what presents. There is nothing that you can do to speed up your realisation of who you are. Life is not an obstacle to knowing truth. Thoughts that you think are yours are not yours at all. That ownership idea arises from your belief that you exist as a separate entity. Thoughts that you want to get it right, and work it out, and abide in the Self, are just mind doing its thing—generating desires. To think that you need time, silence or any condition for spiritual knowledge to unfold within you is an attitude that does not serve. There are no thoughts that are of a higher quality than others—that too is a concept. All thoughts just pass through. Whether you make them yours or not is your play in the scheme of things. The discovery of spiritual knowledge is not a new project for your distraction.

Bypass these mind games and be empty: remain quiet and stop being a thinker.

Should the response arise in you that self-enquiry is a lonely exercise, should you think that solitude is part of this unfolding, then know that the concept of solitude and the experience of solitude are created by mind. The Self has no place for solitude, nothing is separate from it. Remember that Self cannot make mistakes, but mind can. It is only when you identify yourself as someone who can be affected by experiences, as someone whose existence is dependent on how things happen, that suffering presents. Your being is Bliss. It always was. If you are still, your mind may stop seeking your attention. With a pure and quiet mind, the truth of your nature is all that remains. Through self-enquiry, in direct experience of the Self, it is as though you go back to where you never left. In seeing that you are the first and the last, prior and beyond, it is clear that the light of this direct knowledge cannot make you anything.

Chapter 9
EFFORTLESS

Actions that take place from emptiness cannot be actions without love. One does not consciously practice doing the loving thing. In the pure mind, an urge arises and action takes place. In total harmony, selfless giving takes place without motivation, demonstration or expectation, as these are simply thoughts arising. Remain thoughtless, egoless, without the personal, and a universal understanding prevails. There is no one to give, no one to receive—just movements taking place in form. Settle in the freedom of understanding that individuality is only a concept. This is referred to in many monotheistic traditions in statements like "...surrender personal will to divine will...be the hands and feet of God...serving the will of God." These too are signposts that are often read intellectually only, and their true meaning is lost. There cannot be a personal "I" who becomes an instrument of God, because then there are two. And two always brings suffering, as the concept of two can only rise with identification with thought. As long as there is "someone" who is doing, is serving, is acting, no matter how pure the motives, this "someone" cannot be without an agenda. This is the nature of mind. An individual only exists within a mind-created subjective reality. It is entirely natural to live without the personal "I", and to live with it is a troublesome state.

On demonstrating compassion, an outcome is always expected. Even when the action itself is pure, mind has an investment. It is only when without ego, and there is no individual, that the act of absolute compassion takes place through your form. From emptiness, selfless giving takes place. It is then that there is nothing personal in such actions and it is impossible not to act without love. Operating from ideas, one has an option to be kind and loving. All choice comes from mind, totally influenced by one's beliefs in right and wrong. Without thought-identification compassion happens, kindness happens, generosity happens, care and tenderness happen. What flows through naturally is not edited by mind before, during or after—there is no mind involved where there is emptiness.

Giving from total emptiness within seeks no gratitude and leaves no trace or debt in memory as there is no "one", no individual with a sense of "I", engaged in the act of giving. All the values that you hold about being a good person and having a caring attitude are simply thoughts, and the nobler the thought the more attachment there tends to be. Value systems are simply conditioned beliefs. Whatever your lessons in life have been, they now serve to drag the dead past as a reservoir of thought keeping you in bondage. All values and codes of behaviour, all commentaries on the values and behaviours of others, are concepts and judgements, nothing more. They can only keep you trapped. Do not pay respect to that which is held in your mind. All thoughts are subjective, changeable and personal. Let what is moving, move; without your interest, thoughts pass by. Pay no attention to them and, in doing so, your actions will leave no trace of a personal agenda.

In the pure, thoughtless mind, what is natural to the human condition will be cultivated. It is our nature to be loving and kind. Such qualities manifest spontaneously from within. When mind is set aside, humans become kind. Without motivation or conditioned beliefs that speak of doing the right thing, actions take place through your form spontaneously. It is the nature of humankind to be kind. When such actions happen through one who is empty, the optimum order of harmony is at play. For the purpose of communication, this is presented here as a concept. Know it is so beyond conceptual form.

Absolute Reality is not within your body—your body is within Absolute Reality. All that has form happens within that which is. All thoughts arise within it and all identification with thought takes place within it also. You cannot be outside Absolute Reality as you are Absolute Reality. All that can seem to happen is mistaking identity. Then one forgets home for what can be a long time. That too is a thought. But for all, this illusionary state runs out of fuel sooner or later. Thus, one can only be part of the unfolding of consciousness, whether living from the natural state or living a personal life. The personal always gives rise to what seems like disharmony. Yet disharmony only happens within what is harmonious, and cannot be otherwise. The totally harmonious state of all that is remains undisturbed. What is viewed as disharmony is only viewed as such by mind. Thoughts are subtle, and every thought that is entertained as real places you back in the drama of your personal story.

However, as long as there is "I", "me" and "mine", restlessness is present. Here there is choice. You can observe agitation and see you are that which recognises it, knowing that any amount of unrest can be present. You are not that which you can observe. On the other hand, if you are holding fast to the belief that your personal "I" is responsible for the unfolding of your life, that you are the one making it happen, then it may be best to remain with your personal identity for now. Fear will come because you are at the mercy of your thoughts. If personal identity is strong, you will not see the total harmony flowing through your life. It is only strong identification with the personal "I" that blocks your vision. Mind may even tell you that you have evidence that your life illustrates a lack of harmony. Such seductive thoughts always audition for your attention. Observe the play, see disharmony unfolding within perfect harmony, and remain as Absolute freedom.

If you stop engaging the relative perspective, the moment that you cease relative seeing, the relative "you" also ceases. You are the origin of all that can be understood, felt, or thought. So, if you are the origin of the thinker, be the origin and stop pretending to be other than what you are. It is foolish and painful to identify as the thinker or as your thoughts. In truth you are all of it: you cannot separate yourself from what manifests, but to identify with any of it brings suffering. Be what you are, be the origin of all. If you do not think, then who you think you are ends. The thinker, the "I", is always on the move looking for something—a feeling or an experience. As long as you identify as "I", you will try to get the best out of manifestation. You will try to make the best out of life and to get the optimum return. You will look eternally for something from someone that can give you what you think you need. This cycle has no resolution as it is based on the idea that there is something you need and that will help you to get more out of life. While there is nothing wrong with this stream of thought, for starters realise intellectually that this cycle cannot satisfy. The needy and greedy nature of the mind ensures that an unending flux surrounds the personal "I." You can step off of this merry-go-round and abide in Self. In seeing that there is no resolution to the idea of you, and there is no happy-ever-after to the story of the mind, then a total and perfect happiness arises in the death of what you thought you were. If you see the cyclical nature of mind, personal drama ends. When you see that it actually cannot end, then you are out of it—your "I" disappears. What you thought you are ends. The ending of the relative perspective inevitably brings the end of the relative "I".

There is not a single thought that you can have that helps sustain what you are. Nothing you can say or do can make you more of what you are, and there is nothing that can detract. Only your thoughts about yourself manifesting as your image are subject to volatile change. Nothing sustains you or impacts upon you—you are untouchable and beyond all this. No amount of self-defending your position in any situation of circumstance can impact upon you. All physical and mental energy invested in these ideas is just the play of consciousness working out. It can be dropped at any time with immense relief as the relaxation that is enjoyed in the I AM state arises.

Absolute Reality is always present, and when the personal is active (through identification with thought) only a relative reality can be experienced.

Thought takes over and perceiving becomes subjective and illusory. This relative reality creates all the unrest that exists. All global and local disturbance stems from the thoughts of "I" and "me." The common phrase "living in the real world" is in fact referring to the unreal world, the world of thoughts that know no rest. Absolute Reality can only be directly experienced and not fully explained. One by one, all will come to the realisation of this for themselves as consciousness continues to unfold.

In the beginning, effort is required until you tilt the balance resulting in less identification with thoughts than observing periods. Effort is required initially to remember to place your attention in the I AM as observer, because a habit of thought identification must be broken. The mind is used to having free reign and it must be retrained. Most importantly, note that the mind cannot retrain the mind—and it will try to do so.

Your mind turns outward to fulfil desires. In understanding the derivation and role of desires, you begin to turn the mind inward. Be quiet physically and mentally. Without desires and attachment to an object or an outcome, you will taste tremendous love and happiness. When you stop looking outside and want truth above all else, you will see that the outward and inward focus of the mind are the same. Any seeming differences are a conceptual creation of mind. Both inward and outward orientation of mind will cease to exist. Then there is only that which is and all manifestation arises from that.

All spiritual practice arises from a sense of needing to do something—to fix or change what you are. This is generally supported by a work ethic. A sense of being the one who is doing spiritual practice is always present in this effort. Identification with body and mind is also present. The most auspicious purpose to all spiritual practice is to ask, "Who is practising?" Find the origin of the one who is engaged in the practice. As long as there is a sense of you who is doing, no matter how noble the cause, you will seek reward. Ego tries to ensure its continuation, and its motives for action are self-centred. If it does not seek approval from other people, it can seek approval from God. Such is the play of ego. Meditation and spiritual practice help to remove old habits. They do not take you to freedom. If they did, freedom would be dependent on a practice— and it is not. Both the concept of effort and the habit of practice must be removed to recognise that freedom is already here, and what is now here needs nothing. The believed thought that you are not free gives rise to such efforts.

The highest attainment possible through spiritual practice is in reaching the state of experiencing the I AM as I AM. Here, non-identification incubates and there is peace and natural joy, together with freedom from thought and personal identification. Beyond this, the idea that there is one who is engaged in spiritual practice must be dropped, because in the I AM the potential for identifying with experience and thought activity is always present. Belief in being the one who is the doer of all activities is the result of thoughts that arise from your identification with body and mind functioning. Thus, one who engages in spiritual discipline places their idea of what they think is right and proper in front of the unfolding of the universe. Drop the highly revered concept of choice and let it be replaced by recognition of the divine order in manifestation. You can effortlessly know the peace of being carried by a natural flow. All unfolds without your help. Should thoughts come to challenge this, recognise them for what they are. Be the detached observer who is without judgement or preference. In this natural state, you are not manipulating anything and you enjoy a delightful indifference towards all that takes place.

Desires can be fulfilled or not fulfilled; it is wise to expect this to go either way. Know that things might or might not happen; therein ends the problem of desires. All pursued desires ultimately lead to pain. Even the desire for love must eventually lead to loss and sorrow. It is better to transcend both love and sorrow: that is to accept them both equally. Understand such dualistic changeful dynamics to be the manifestation of the nature of life. In abandoning desires, you are enabled to walk freely among manifestation as desire is the greatest pollutant of the mind. Behind every experience, peace remains unchanged. Let experience itself be perceived. No experience can create impact on what you are. From the egoic personal position, all experiences are loaded with pleasure and pain. It follows that all is turbulent. Perhaps the most engaging activity for the mind is sex and, even in the most consuming moments of the sexual act, you can observe that your body, your emotions and your chemistry are fully embracing this experience, yet your mind can be perfectly still and resting in complete emptiness. This may not be the easiest place to start, but the point remains so. In every moment and no matter what the situation, you can bring your attention to that which observes. As this becomes automatic, you will not have to remind yourself to do so. No matter where you are, and no matter what you are doing, you can observe.

Making this a project or something to do is missing the point. It is effortless. Do not fool yourself into thinking that you have to work something out in order to be what you already are. Effortlessly, you are

That. Stay in quiet observance of any resistance in your mind. You may see how thoughts do not intrude on the underlying peace of your natural state. Let your mind be in total chaos. Your levels of thought activity are of no significance. Do not lose your attention in the story of any thought, and thoughts will subside. You are That which watches all. Recognise this, and peace alone prevails. Mind is insignificant and it does not need to behave for the Absolute to be. Mind will never assist its own downfall. Switch off from all struggle and it passes naturally. There is no attitude to adopt and there are no tricks. It all unfolds in the recognition, and effortless recognition takes place without your assistance. Inner alignment happens and harmonisation takes place by itself. To want this to happen is simply an engagement with thought. Stop engaging with thoughts and do not make this disengagement with thoughts something to do!

The mind loves distraction. It continually seeks to be involved in doing something. It can be obsessed with ideas of what to do and what not to do, and what to do after this...and then what...and then what... Thoughts of what to do are seductive. Doing something is easier than not doing. Pushing yourself to do hard work, to practice, to make deadlines, is easier than sitting still. Mind loves activity. The doer that is ego wants to act according to its rules of conduct. Doing what you think you should do, what you think will make you or others happy, or what you think is expected of you must be dropped. These compulsions arise from a desire to control, and appear to prevent other things from happening. Observe this fear and let it all happen.

Fear arises for most at this point. Your mind can create great fear to escape the truth. Mind does not want to be redundant. It does not like to serve you instead of directing you. So expect fear to present at the most likely opportunities for realising the Absolute Self. It does not matter what the fear is about, as all fear is founded on your conditioning and is therefore total rubbish. But some thoughts are given so much reverence and attention that, every time one is presented as truthful and convincing, you offer respect by giving it all your attention. When you identify with a persistent thought or fear you merge with it, and when you are one with something you cannot see it. Objectivity is lost for a while. Realise this and let it get as bad as it can become. Let what is going to happen, happen and let what mind can throw at you come too. Mind presents threats and ideas in rapid succession. It can play dirty, but call its bluff and you will see that it has no power beyond the chaotic movement of thoughts. You can identify with them or not. The same system applies. Mind has no other tools to hold you in bondage.

When great fear arises, that within you that recognises fear is not fearful. If you can observe fear, then you are not playing victim to this emotion. Place your attention on that which sees fear. From this objective perspective, the thought of fear is no more potent than the thought of a butterfly. Observe and be that which is not fearful, that which is unchanging, reactionless and undisturbed. Fear comes and goes. If you are not attached to it, it will pass. The only staying power available is that which is offered by your attention. This is effortless. If you apply effort, your attention is with thoughts. You do not have to control your emotions, senses or feelings. Observe them. Let all that is unfolding, unfold. Let all experiences roll out, and be the perceiving of this unfolding. The Ultimate Seer is not unfolding: it simply is and you are That. You are what was before all sensations that can arise. It is simple and natural to let what is passing, pass. Place your attention on what is here and not moving. Behind every emotion, there is nothingness. Do not feel this as an experience. Because if you feel emptiness as an experience, then mind is active and will soon replace emptiness with fear. This is not about feeling emptiness, it is being emptiness. You cannot try to be it, you are it. You cannot think your way into emptiness, you can only think your way into your thoughts. The golden key here is effortlessness. After all, what is natural requires no technique and no action on your part. Switch off your interest in the movie of your mind, no matter how realistic it appears. Stop actively thinking. Sink into what is unchanging. This is not something to do. It is effortless as it is the not doing of anything that invites the natural state to present in your consciousness. Effortlessly, be that which observes all, and then go to where Ultimate Seeing stems from. Be there and rest there. Totally natural!

Mind likes to categorise and create contexts. Do not fall into the trap that, when you are working, you cannot impartially observe. (The only time you cannot observe is when something has interfered with your ability to be conscious, such as sustained head injury, fainting, certain drugs etc.) Many find that once they stopped identifying with their role in the workplace and removed the personal agenda, a natural detachment from colleagues took place. New understandings of how they functioned became clear. This is not self-enquiry but personal development, and it too has its place. Impartial observation enables seeing things as they are. In the beginning, this can be mistaken for the natural state. The idea of watching or observing in this way is part of personal identification. It is laden with judgement. It is an activity of mind with a commentary.

Go beyond this, because in this example the perceiver of the story is also part of the story. Observing and judging, observing and realising, observing and gaining new understandings of how you are is not self-enquiry. This is simply mind engaged in analysis. Be that which sees what is seeing. Do not be the watcher. You are That which sees that which is watching. Observing the observer is a peacefully exquisite and effortless natural state. Something within, That which you are, does not need to apply change, to do, to fulfil, to judge or to practice. It is harmonious and enjoys the total freedom of choicelessness.

To choose is mind, to allow is mind, to serve is mind. Replacing one set of principles for another is a mind game. Know that mind is not an enormous faculty to manage. It is a facility that enables you to experience. Like your senses, let it serve you and not rule you. In the effortless neutrality of your natural state, all doubts, fears and anxieties vanish: they only come back to serve you. Let understanding happen. There is nothing for you to intellectually figure out. There is no final experience that brings things to a natural conclusion. There is no "how to remain in the Self." You are the Self. This question is like asking, "How do you remain a human?" Without any effort, the nature of being human is within you. Mind volunteers to step up to the task of abiding in the Self, but there is no task. You are already Self. There is nothing to do to be more of what you are. You are synonymous with what is Absolute: you are not your personality—the one you call "I." In recognising this, there is a wonderful sense that you are free from the grip of mind. In recognising that you are prior to all concepts, you will see that you had no beginning and you have no end. You are what you are and always have been That. Whatever arises will fall. There is no action, feeling, emotion or thought that does not stand on the foundation of Absolute Self, and there is no moment when Absolute Self is not.

When the ego performs activities, these are also acts of the Absolute playing through the form of the personal "I" who is the doer. All resulting actions have a price tag, as this arises from the density of identification. What happens is that you impose the notion of personally-performed activity—in this case "I am doing this"—on the natural substratum of inactivity and stillness. The Absolute is not busy. In total emptiness and joy, there is inactivity. From the Absolute rises the notion of activity and, as long as a personal "I" is at large, you will get involved in activity. If you attach to the idea that you are the doer, you are lost in another story. In addition, this adds turbulence to the perfectly harmonious flow. If you truly understand and can confirm where from all activity arises, you will see it arises from non-action. Within That which is beyond activation, there is infinite freedom. Do not move from this state to identify with the one who loves to do. Now, all action takes place simply and purely through your form and cannot register in a personal memory. It is then that the world will not be troubled by you.

Chapter 10
NOTHING IS

That which is Absolute has no way of being separate from you. All comes from the Absolute, stays as Absolute, and merges back into the Absolute. No matter what the expression in form or formless, all that is remains Absolute. Your individuality is an expression of that which is beyond individuality. Individuality is the illusion that you are not identical with the Absolute. Drop the illusion and only Absolute remains. There is no separation. Be without the idea of individuality and, from that which remains, something reveals itself. All manifestation appears from the Absolute and is moved by an arising power, but the Absolute is not the creator. The Absolute never acts and is without desire or will. The term Absolute is a concept when expressed in consciousness. It is a synonym for the immanent reality discovered with realisation of the Self.

The I AM state is part of all that comes and goes. It remains present as long as you have a physical body (there are rare exceptions). While you can transcend the ego by throwing off all identification with thought, the sense I AM stays. It offers an intuitive sense of "I" without identification with ego. This sense of "I"—referred to as I AM—is useful for the functioning, as a human being. The I AM is not present in deep sleep, and is not required once the vital force ceases to support your physical body. After physical death, whatever thought-identification remains, the beliefs held to be true will pull another state into existence for you to continue experiencing. Thus, you will continue to have experiences in another dimension (afterlife) or reincarnate according to your beliefs, be they conscious or unconscious. The underpinning belief is always the same however—the next dimension or experience will bring the happiness I want. This is dependency and it can continue for a very long time while nothing ever happens; Self remains unchanged. The cycle continues until identification with thought ceases permanently and it is realised that Self alone exists. There is nothing external other than illusory thought.

The cycle of birth and death pertains to your body and only holds significance for you for as long as you believe you are your body. When you realise that you are free from the illusion of body and mind identification, you will know no death. Death applies to the physical form only. On realising the Self, your innocent body is insignificant to your beingness. You are it all, there is no place you are not, and you are not subject to time. Mind perceives form and names it as different to what you are. This is the erroneous use of mind. Nothing ever happened to you. You are Absolute Self playing through form. You were never born and you cannot die. The cycle of birth and death is a device of the ego mind. As long as the ego engages in activity, it can comprehend the phrase that you were born to be free. You were never born, there is nothing to gain, and you were never free or not free. You are beyond all of this and beyond the concept of freedom. When the ego is dropped, this cycle ends also.

You are Self and Self sees nothing apart from Self. From Self arises the first thought of intuitive "I" or I AM, and Self remains in perfect stillness and is unchanging. If you enquire as to the root of this original thought, you will find that it does not exist. If you have taken this step, then how can you continue to be deluded by what you know to be false? It is said that forgetting the Self is what makes enjoyment of creation possible. It is only for the sake of play and celebration that Self is forgotten or appears to be forgotten. Creation continuously unfolds within consciousness. It is real and unreal at the same time. The world and all its forms come from the Absolute in which there is nothing. Through your thoughts, you made what is unreal real to you. In truth, there is no creation and no experiencer, yet there appear to be experiences and one who has experiences. This is a paradox for mind only because, without identification, there is no difference between subject and object.

The world and mind play together. Of these two, the world owes its appearance to the mind alone. The world cannot exist independently of your mind, so how can the world be other than mind? Thus, how you see the world is how you see yourself. The world is not problematic. The idea you have about yourself is where the mistake lies. Thus, your perspective on the world is erroneous. All that has physical form derives its existence from thought. Relativity underpins all manifestation. The world is founded on the substratum of ego. It comprises the perceived and named objects of your senses. Yet enquiry reveals that ego does not exist. Therefore, all that is based on ego does not exist either. But so long as your mind copulates with your imaginings, creation will continue to go on for you. All presenting in manifestation was created by you, and it will be destroyed by you, on transcending mind. Both mind and world rise and fall within Reality that never moves.

Avoid creating a concept of Self. There can only be a signpost to That which is beyond. It is not at a distance from you. To reach for it implies that your mind thinks it exists physically and can be attained. Therefore, it cannot be immanent. Drop all such concepts and rest. Be still, quiet and patient. There is only you. How can there be a distance between you and you? You simply imagined a plethora of ideas arising from you to placate an identity that pulled you into its story. There is nothing to trip your footing now apart from your own thinking. Make use of all that comes and do not complain. Recognise that that which you fear is mere thought and prove it inwardly. Stay as the formless witness. All you have feared at any time in your life is no more than a thought that you believed into existence. Things that you imagined to be so are no more than imaginings. If you accept that mind exists, you will try to control it and manage it. This is mind trying to control mind. If you self-enquire as to whether mind exists at all, you will find that it does not. Mind itself is simply a thought. This discovery brings freedom.

Absolute or Self alone exists. There is nothing external to That. Effortlessly drop the thought of things being external. The Absolute is imperishable and does not have attributes. Absolute is pure existence, pure knowledge, pure consciousness, pure beauty and pure happiness. Absolute is pure silence, pure stillness, pure joy and pure bliss. These are not qualities, but substances themselves beyond concepts of substance. Absolute is Ultimate and Reality. This cannot be experienced phenomenally. You cannot dip in and out of what you are. But the inner confirming and deep understanding that you are the Absolute is unmistakable. Enquire within and prove it to yourself.

The Absolute does not decide where attention should go. There is no intention or attention. You only ever had the illusion that you decide what to experience. Once this is seen, there is a sense of surrendering into what IS. This natural effortlessness arises from the state of no resistance and is pure freedom. If you think you can control your actions or experiences, all you are doing is gathering stories to consolidate the sense of "me" and "mine." What difference does what you perceive and what you experience make? If you believe you can change any of it, that is a thought. Only ego cares about your intentions and attention. Celebrate that you cannot control anything. If you deeply understand this, you will not continue to impose limitations on yourself and then make a vain struggle to transcend them. Ignore the ego and you are free: nothing else is needed. Stop reasoning. Do not engage in identification and the rest is effortless. There is nothing new to be gained and nothing remains to be accomplished. Tendencies, habits, limitations were all incorrectly assumed as real. In truth there is no need to transcend them. What can you gain by attributing your misery to the happenings in your life? This is the play of erroneous ideas. All phenomena come and go, Absolute never stirs. Thus, realise that salvation is permanent and mind is no more than a myth.

Enquire within, go to the root of the primary thought and stay there. In the natural state, there is no awareness of difference: the world as God validates itself as truth. There is nothing apart from you, all that you see around you is you. The world reveals itself as the kingdom of heaven and it is within you.

In the Absolute, peace and joy are felt. This most natural state has completeness and totality. Do not make this an experience. If you do, it will pass as the identification with one who experiences is activated. Peace and joy are natural. This is what you are. Know this to be so without the subjective egoic perspective of an experiencer having an experience. In the natural state, all bodily senses function as normal, the phenomenal world can be observed, and activities unfold as usual. All that passes is observed from the unchanging peace and happiness that is Self. Among that which is fully understood to be transient, there can be pleasure and physical pain. These are a part of life and there is no attachment to or preference for any state. There are no identifications with, or judgements of, daily activities as they unfold. The natural state is not interested in labels, phenomena and outcomes. Naming of events ceases. Thus, there is in fact no event—and it follows that nothing happens.

The natural state is empty. Without the mental application of naming all that changes, movement only appears to take place. There is absolute clarity that nothing is happening. Without the egoic personal "I," an intuitive sense of "I" from emptiness functions throughout each day. There are no thoughts that ask, "What should I do?" in any situation, as mind is concerned with matters of responsibility, but somehow all things are addressed. The activity that arises out of emptiness is more efficient than that which is per-

115

formed from the laden identification with one who is doing. From the natural state, there is no recognition of that "one", and it is recognised that the vital force, Self, Source, God, the Absolute is performing all activities. That vital force is what you are and you were never other than That. There is an apparent coming and going observed from the natural state. It appears as movement and happening of events. If the universal flow directs the unfolding of a great happening though your form, then you will rise to it. If the order of things creates a burning urge within you to make local or global change happen, then you will flow with that urge. If you are not stirred into activity while remaining in the stillness of no mind, then no activity takes place. There is no feeling that you are either participating or not participating in any action. Nothing is named and all movement comes out of pure emptiness. Without mind, without being the one involved in doing, there is no personal agenda attaching to activity. Through action or inaction, you cannot but be of service to that which is manifesting in consciousness. Expectations and desired outcomes do not exist now.

If you recognise that consciousness plays out laughter and anger, great deeds and horrendous violence, then you are the witness of it. You are free. Now without effort, from the I AM, mind slips into the original state, identification with thoughts does not happen, and you return to emptiness. The revelation that every thing that can happen in creation is simply consciousness playing out, dissolves the personal "I." Once realised, this revelation cannot change, it cannot be lost or taken from you. With time, it stabilises within you. Intuitively, you recognise you are the Absolute unchanging and still. All that moves and changes cannot be you, but rather an appearance arising and falling in time and space. Whatever arises must be preceded by that which is there to see it. From the natural state, all is effortlessly perceived and not actively watched. Your realisation is here now. What you are IS and nothing needs to happen.

The Absolute never lost itself. Absolute was never and cannot be part of the story created by thought. Your nature was never involved in the dramas of your imagination. You cannot be less by forgetting the Self, you cannot be more by remembering your natural state. Forgetting happens and you can suffer if you imagine that you have forgotten Self. This happens in consciousness. The Absolute is not something you must remember in order for it to be. Suffering can arise only from believing the thought that you have forgotten. In spite of everything, you cannot get closer or further from what you are. All of this is imaginary.

You are not something you can loose, and thus you cannot attain who you are through experience. Your nature is not dependent on how you experience yourself. You can experience yourself in any way possible—hate yourself, love yourself. It does not matter. Your nature is not dependent on this. All that can be experienced is the idea of you as an experiencer experiencing yourself. If you desire to become more of what you are, suffering ensues, as all such efforts consolidate the existence of an experiencer experiencing separation. Your nature does not have to be aware in order to be what it is, neither does it need you to be aware. Self does not have to be aware of itself to be blissful happiness. Be that which is Pure Awareness, that which does not need.

Consciousness gives rise to great visions and to unsavoury fracas equally without preference. Accept and witness all of the play—nothing can bind you. In this stillness, you have no enemies, no attachments, no subjective thoughts or judgements. Recognise internally that the universe moves through you. Allow it to be the only force that moves you.

If that which is presented in this book is becoming clear for you, if you feel you are getting closer to something, you are simply deluded by the clever workings of your mind. If you think there is something to accomplish then you must believe that you are not the Self. When you imagine that you forget Self, you see and name objects from the perspective of you as subject. Stay as Self and you will not see the objective world: there is only the subject. The concepts presented here are but the faintest shadow of That which does not need to be clear or accomplished in any way. It does not need to be understood to be, not even by you who is That.

Be in your natural state here and now. If you believe that you cannot, it is better to forget it altogether. Thoughts of there being another place and time that would support this for you are from your mind, as it creates new beliefs that will manifest as your reality. There is no journey for you to travel, no shift for you to make from ego to Self, as this requires two and, therefore, is just another thought. Curiosity will not help you. When a natural desire arises from your heart and it becomes an emergency to know the truth, it is then that resistance ceases to play in you and Self will begin to shine forth.

Happiness is the Self. When you sink into it, what is found is pure happiness that does not come to an end. When mind merges in the Self, there is only fullness, completeness—and that is the state of bliss. Thus, the bliss that is enjoyed unconsciously in deep sleep is enjoyed consciously in abiding in the Self. The expression of Self is love, and the manifestation of Self is the manifestation of Grace in existence. Self is Grace. It is absurd to think that it can be acquired from others. It is what you are. Grace does not manifest where identification with thought is present, but as mind merges in Self, Grace gushes forth.

All this book can offer are signposts and an intellectual perspective. To see your destination, you must stop looking at signposts and place your attention on that to which is indicated. What is offered here has been reduced to concepts that you must set aside. Spiritual knowledge must be directly experienced. It is time to embody the truth and stop talking and reading about it. All your intellect can do is measure variety, and how can you measure Self? It would be an easier task to measure the sky. Do not be bothered by what is real and what is not real: it is time to transcend these and all concepts. The egoic mind likes to talk about the truth. This is another distraction, an avoidance of abiding in the Self. Be quiet and merge in Self, consciously. Be the embodiment of Self and a great force emanating peace, joy, harmony and love will surround your very presence. This is the greatest gift to humanity, but please do not take my word for it—prove it to be so.

Breinigsville, PA USA
07 December 2009
228814BV00003B/1/P